To Chris and Jos
XO Cole

I LOVE BACON!

I LOVE

JAYNE ROCKMILL

PHOTOGRAPHY BY
BEN FINK

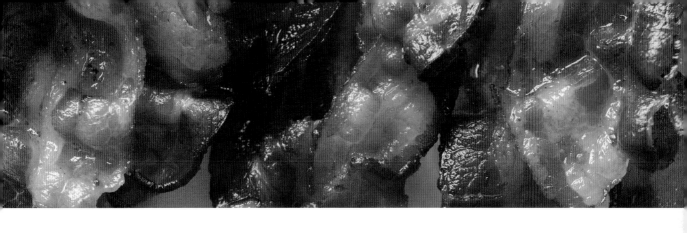

BACON!

Andrews McMeel
Publishing, LLC
Kansas City · Sydney · London

10 11 12 13 14 SDB 10 9 8 7 6 5 4 3 2 1

ISBN: 978-0-7407-9766-8

Library of Congress Control Number: 2010927149

Design: Vertigo Design, NYC
Photography: Ben Fink
Food styling: Jaime Kimm
Prop styling: Roy Finamore

Jasper White's recipe for Egg Chowder with Bacon and New Potatoes was previously published in *50 Chowders: One Pot Meals—Clam, Corn, and Beyond*, Scribner, 2000. It is used here with permission.

A portion of the royalties from sales of this book will be donated to Food Bank for New York and Share Our Strength. For more on these charities, see page 122.

www.andrewsmcmeel.com

Attention: Schools And Businesses
Andrews McMeel books are available at quantity discounts with bulk purchase for educational, business, or sales promotional use. For information, please write to: Special Sales Department, Andrews McMeel Publishing, LLC, 1130 Walnut Street, Kansas City, Missouri 64106.

CONTENTS

Who doesn't love bacon? You don't even

have to eat it to love it. Ask a vegetarian what he or she misses most, and chances are good that it's bacon. Thomas Jefferson was a bacon lover, and legendary foodie James Beard sang its praises when he wrote, "There are few sights that appeal to me more than the streaks of lean and fat in a good side of bacon, or the lovely round of pinkish meat framed in delicate white fat that is Canadian bacon." Whether it evokes fond memories of hearty home-cooked breakfasts or rich spaghetti carbonara dinners, bacon has happy associations.

Bacon is remarkably versatile. Few foods are as satisfying when munched on their own or have the ability to enhance the flavor of so many other foods the way that bacon does. It's used in literally everything from soup (Roasted Tomato and Smoked Bacon Bisque) to nuts (Chocolate-Dipped Smoked Almond Bacon Brittle). If you are a serious connoisseur, check out the Making Your Own Bacon chapter, with its recipes for Classic Cured Bacon, Chinese-Style Pork Belly, and more.

In fact, bacon is popular all over the world. You will find that it comes with a variety of names and from different parts of the pig. Pancetta is from the pork belly but is cured only, not smoked; Canadian bacon is pork loin; guanciale is from the cheek; and British bacon is the back fat. In the United States, bacon is most often associated with iconic foods like the BLT, but it is also a key ingredient in cuisines as diverse as Italian pastas, Spanish tapas, Thai stir-fries, and Mexican tacos. In this book, you will find that bacon is a great complement to every food group: dairy, grains, vegetables, fish, and meat.

In the Alps, the hearty potato- and bacon-based tartiflette has been around for centuries, and the French have been adding bacon to their quiches since the sixteenth century! Compared to these venerable dishes, the good ol' American BLT is just a baby, having become popularized only when fresh lettuce and tomatoes became available year-round with the rapid expansion of supermarkets after World War II. In this book you will find two updated versions of the BLT. Monica Byrne replaces typical mayonnaise with a roasted red pepper aïoli and toast with focaccia, whereas Ellen Burke Van Slyke uses sun-dried tomatoes, a Meyer lemon aïoli, and brioche and cuts the sandwiches into cocktail-size bites.

The collection of recipes here captures everything we love about bacon. Bacon has a crunchy texture, a sublime smoky flavor, an ability to bring out the best in other foods, and an incomparably irresistible aroma. As Doug Larson, a gold medalist in the 1924 Olympics, observed, "Life expectancy would grow by leaps and bounds if green vegetables smelled as good as bacon."

When I first began this project, my intention was to help the hungry in a creative way. For years I have passionately joined forces with the many organizations that work so tirelessly to abolish hunger in America. It also helped that I, too, am a foodie. Combining my two passions has allowed me to take this journey. With the cooperation and generosity of many inspiring chefs, this bacon book has evolved into what you have in your hands. My hope is that you will enjoy the journey as much as I have. Whether you think bacon is just part of a good BLT or whether you are daring enough to try bacon in a chocolate cupcake, let us all remember that when we open our minds to trying new things, we become part of change. Proceeds from the sale of this book will be donated to Food Bank for New York City and Share Our Strength. In keeping hope alive, these donations will help bring about the most needed change. Thank you for your support, and as the saying goes, "It takes a village!"

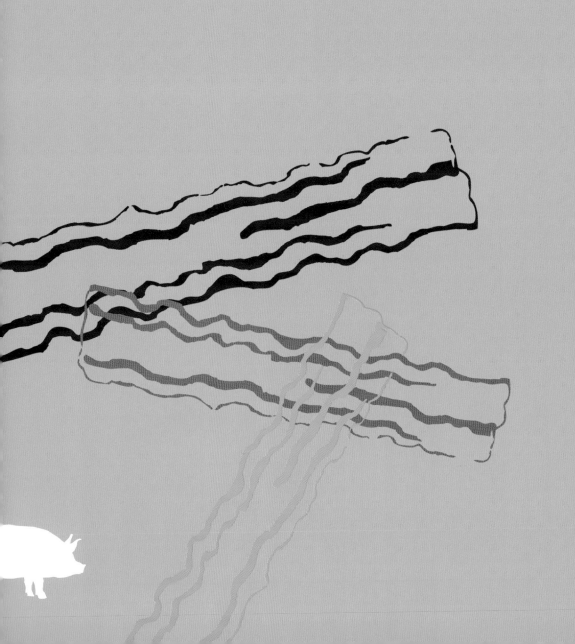

MAKE YOUR OWN BACON

Classic Cured Bacon 3
Spicy Braised Bacon 4
Soy-Ginger Braised Bacon 5
Crispy Pork Belly 6
Chinese-Style Pork Belly 7

CLASSIC CURED BACON

Makes 2 to 3 pounds

½ cup dark brown sugar
½ cup kosher salt
¼ cup pink (or curing) salt

¾ teaspoon black peppercorns, cracked and coarsely ground in a mortar and pestle
1 (2-pound) pork belly, skin on

In a medium bowl, combine the brown sugar, kosher salt, pink salt, and pepper and mix well. Pour the mixture onto a work surface and roll the pork belly in it to completely coat it. Place in a seal-able storage container, seal tightly, and store in the refrigerator for 1 week.

Preheat the oven to 300°F. Place the pork belly in a roasting pan or on a baking sheet. Cover with parchment paper and aluminum foil and bake until the internal temperature registers 156°F on a meat thermometer. This should take about 1 hour. Remove from the oven, place on a wire rack, and allow to cool in the refrigerator.

The bacon will keep for weeks covered tightly in the refrigerator. Slice off pieces as needed to use in your favorite recipes.

NOTE: *Of course, you can purchase smoked bacon from your local butcher, but try this recipe. It may seem like a lengthy process, but once you have the cured bacon, you can head in so many directions, from simply slicing it and enjoying it with crusty bread to using it to tasty effect in a fantastic salad. In fact, it's great in the Grilled Bacon and Cucumber Salad with Chili Caramel Dressing (page 49). The crispy smoked bacon goes well with the sweet yet spicy chili caramel for a salad that's welcome year-round.*

SPICY BRAISED BACON

Makes 2 pounds

1 meaty boneless pork belly (about 2 pounds), skinned

1 tablespoon freshly ground black pepper

1 tablespoon crushed red chili flakes

1 tablespoon coriander seeds

1 tablespoon fennel seeds

Kosher salt

Vegetable oil, for sautéing

1 medium white onion, coarsely chopped

1 fennel head, quartered

1 large carrot, coarsely chopped

1 stalk celery, coarsely chopped

A few sprigs of rosemary

A few sprigs of thyme

2 bay leaves

2 cups San Marzano tomatoes (see Note)

2 cups white wine

2 gallons pork or beef stock

Portion the pork belly into 6 equal-size pieces. In a spice grinder, combine the black pepper, chili flakes, coriander seeds, and fennel seeds and finely grind them. Season the pork belly with salt, then rub with the spice rub. Let it marinate overnight in the refrigerator.

Preheat the oven to 325°F.

Heat the oil in a large stockpot over medium heat. Add the onion, fennel, carrot, celery, rosemary sprigs, thyme sprigs, and bay leaves and sauté for about 20 minutes. Once the vegetables are cara-melized, add the tomatoes, cook for 25 minutes, then deglaze with the white wine. Once the liquid is reduced by three-quarters, add the pork or beef stock and cook until the vegetables are tender, about 45 minutes.

While the vegetables are cooking, prepare a grill to cook over direct high heat. Grill the pork belly until it begins to render some of its fat and becomes dark golden brown, 8 to 10 minutes, and turn and repeat.

Preheat the oven to 325°F. Stir the vegetables well and then strain the braising liquid into a bowl; discard the vegetables. Transfer the pork belly to a nonreactive ovenproof pan and cover it with the reserved braising liquid. Bake until tender, about 2 hours and 30 minutes. You can use this bacon in your favorite recipes, or try it in the Spagna Beans and Treviso Radicchio recipe on page 47. You'll also need to reserve some of the braising liquid for that recipe. Tightly sealed cured bacon keeps in the refrigerator for up to a month.

NOTE: *San Marzano tomatoes are flavorful plum tomatoes from the San Marzano region of Italy.*

SOY-GINGER BRAISED BACON

Makes 1 pound

1 (1-pound) piece slab bacon, skin on

1 tablespoon olive oil

½ cup chopped fresh ginger

2 shallots, chopped

3 cloves garlic, chopped

¼ cup loosely packed dark brown sugar

1 bay leaf

1 cup soy sauce

3 cups chicken stock

Preheat the oven to 250°F. Gently score the skin side of the bacon with crosshatch marks, being careful not to cut too deep.

Heat a large sauté pan over medium-high heat. When the pan is hot, sear and brown the bacon on all sides, about 2 minutes per side.

Heat the oil in a 5-quart Dutch oven over high heat. Add the ginger and shallots and cook until they soften and the shallots begin to turn translucent, about 5 minutes. Add the garlic and continue to cook for 1 minute. Add the brown sugar. Stir.

When the brown sugar has fully dissolved, add the bay leaf, soy sauce, and chicken stock and bring the mixture to a simmer. Add the bacon and cover the dish with a tight-fitting lid or heavy-duty aluminum foil.

Braise the bacon in the oven for 2 hours and 30 minutes. Set the pot aside for 15 minutes to cool slightly.

Remove the bacon from the Dutch oven and discard the rest of the contents of the pot. Cut the bacon into 4 portions for the recipe on page 67 as a main entrée ingredient or use it in your favorite recipes. You can store the pork belly for up to 1 week in the refrigerator.

CHEF/OWNER "IAN" CHALERMKITTICHAI, **CUISINE CONCEPT CO., LTD., BANGKOK, THAILAND**

CRISPY PORK BELLY

Makes 2 pounds

2 pounds pork belly, skin on

1 tablespoon sea salt

¼ cup white vinegar

Canola oil, for frying

Rinse the pork belly with cold water and put it in a medium stockpot. Cover with cold water, bring to a boil over medium heat, and then simmer for 50 minutes, until tender. Remove the pork belly from the pot and place it skin side up on a small rimmed baking sheet. Let it rest in a cool place for 30 minutes.

Gently score the skin of the pork belly with a paring knife, leaving 1 inch between cuts and being careful not to cut deep down close to the pork fat. Use a fork to prick the skin of the pork belly. Rub the skin with the salt, then pour on the white vinegar. Turn the pork belly skin side down and let it soak for 30 minutes.

Preheat the oven at 400˚F. Bake the pork belly until the skin starts to pop up, about 30 minutes.

In a deep fryer large enough to hold the pork belly, heat the oil to 350º to 375ºF on a deep-frying thermometer. Fry the pork belly until crispy and golden brown, 7 to 10 minutes.

Let it rest for 5 to 7 minutes before slicing, or refrigerate for up to 1 week and slice as needed. You can use this bacon in your favorite recipes, or try it in the Crispy Stir-Fry on page 54.

CHINESE-STYLE PORK BELLY

Makes 2 pounds

2 pounds pork belly (see Note)

3 tablespoons kosher salt

1 tablespoon freshly ground black pepper

4 cups chicken stock

1 cup pineapple juice

½ cup oyster sauce

½ cup soy sauce

½ cup shao hsing rice wine

½ cup packed brown sugar

1½ tablespoons Szechuan peppercorns

3 star anise

¼ cup thinly sliced fresh ginger

1 large onion, quartered

2 cloves garlic, crushed

Cut the pork belly in half. Season both sides with the salt and pepper, wrap it in plastic wrap, and refrigerate overnight.

Heat a large sauté pan over high heat. When the pan is very hot, place the pork belly fat side down in the pan, lower the heat to medium, brown the fat side, then turn the meat over and brown the other side. (There is no need for oil because you are rendering fat from the belly.) Transfer to a large ovenproof pan and repeat with the other piece of pork belly.

Preheat the oven to 300°F. Place the chicken stock, pineapple juice, oyster sauce, soy sauce, shao hsing, brown sugar, Szechuan peppercorns, star anise, ginger, onion, and garlic in a large stockpot and bring to a simmer over medium-high heat. Pour the mixture over the pork belly. Cover the pan with a lid or aluminum foil and bake for 2 hours, until tender.

Let the pork belly cool in the liquid. When cool, remove from the liquid (discard the liquid), slice the belly ¼ inch thick, and refrigerate until ready to use. It will keep, covered, in the refrigerator for up to 1 week.

To serve, heat a nonstick pan over medium heat and cook the slices until crisped to your liking.

NOTE: *If possible, it's best to allow the seasoned pork belly to sit overnight in the refrigerator to allow the salt to penetrate the meat. It should marinate for a minimum of 8 hours.*

BRUNCH

Bakon Mary Cocktail 11

Poached Eggs Wrapped in
Maple-Smoked Bacon Over Lentils 12

Poached Eggs with Bacon, Peas, Mushrooms,
and Truffle Oil 14

Eggs with Vadouvan Fingers and Bacon Emulsion 16

Savory Bacon Bread Pudding 18

Breakfast Pie 20

Bacon, Asparagus, and Gruyère Quiche 21

Mediterranean BLTs 22

BAKON MARY COCKTAIL

Serves 1

1 strip bacon

1 ounce Bakon Vodka

8 ounces (1 cup) tomato juice

1 dash celery salt

1 dash ground black pepper

1 dash Tabasco sauce

2 to 4 dashes Worcestershire sauce

⅛ teaspoon grated horseradish

1 teaspoon freshly squeezed lime juice, plus a lime wedge for wetting the rim of the glass

1 cup ice cubes

½ celery stalk, for garnish

Cook the bacon in a skillet over low heat until crispy, about 10 minutes. Drain on a paper towel. When cool, crumble the bacon into very small pieces and set aside.

Combine the vodka, tomato juice, celery salt, black pepper, Tabasco, Worcestershire, horseradish, and lime juice in a cocktail tumbler. Shake or stir until thoroughly combined.

Use a lime wedge to wet the rim of a highball glass, then dip the top of the glass in the crumbled bacon. Carefully fill the glass with the ice cubes and pour the liquid into the glass. Garnish with the celery stalk and serve.

POACHED EGGS WRAPPED IN MAPLE-SMOKED BACON OVER LENTILS

Serves 4

3 tablespoons rendered bacon fat

3 tablespoons chopped shallot

1 teaspoon chopped garlic, plus 6 whole cloves, peeled

2 tablespoons sherry vinegar, plus a dash for the lentils

½ teaspoon fresh thyme leaves, plus 2 whole sprigs

1 sprig rosemary

3 bay leaves

1 onion, diced

1 stalk celery

1 carrot

½ cup bacon cut into 1-inch pieces

2 cups beluga lentils (see Note)

1 cup dry red wine

2 brown sugar cubes

Salt and freshly ground black pepper

4 large eggs

4 cups peanut oil, for frying

16 thin slices (⅛-inch thick) maple-smoked bacon

2 cups bitter greens, such as arugula

Prepare the vinaigrette. In a medium saucepan over medium heat, melt the bacon fat. Add the shallot and chopped garlic and cook until soft and translucent, about 5 minutes. Remove from the heat, add the 2 tablespoons of sherry vinegar and the thyme leaves, and set aside until ready to serve.

Place the rosemary, thyme sprigs, and bay leaves in a piece of cheesecloth and tie up the bundle with kitchen twine to make a sachet; set aside.

In a food processor, puree the onion, celery, carrot, and the whole garlic cloves until smooth. Set aside.

Put the diced bacon in a 3-quart saucepan over medium heat and cook until the fat is rendered and the bacon begins to color. Add the vegetable puree and cook until soft and sweet, about 10 minutes. Add the lentils and mix, coating them with the vegetables and bacon fat. Add the red wine and sugar and cook until the mixture absorbs the liquid and is dry, about 5 minutes. Add enough water to cover, season with salt and pepper, add the sachet, and bring to a simmer. Cook slowly until the mixture is cooked through but the lentils aren't mushy, about 30 minutes. Adjust the seasoning, if necessary. Add a dash of sherry vinegar, remove the sachet, and set the pot aside in a warm place.

To poach the eggs, fill a small saucepan with about 1 inch of water. Place it over high heat to boil it quickly, then decrease to a simmer. Stir the water clockwise with a spoon to create a swirling effect, then carefully crack an egg and gently slide it into the water so the yolk does not break. Gently spoon water over the egg so the white cooks quickly and covers the yolk. Cook for 1 to 2 minutes, until the white is firm but the yolk is still runny. Use a slotted spoon to gently transfer the egg to a small bowl. Repeat with the remaining eggs, transferring them to separate bowls. Chill the eggs, covered in their bowls, until ready to plate.

Heat the peanut oil in a 4-quart saucepan to 375°F on a deep-frying thermometer. Line 4 cereal bowls with 4 slices of bacon each, overlapping the bacon and covering all sides of the bowls. Place a chilled poached egg into each bacon-lined bowl and gather up the bacon to completely enclose and cover the egg. Fry the bacon and egg packets two at a time (so they are not crowded) until golden and crispy, about 5 minutes.

Spoon some lentils into each of the cereal bowls and place a bacon-wrapped egg in the center of the lentils. Place the greens in a medium bowl, toss with the vinaigrette, and arrange around the eggs on the plate. Serve immediately.

NOTE: *Beluga lentils are caviar-size black lentils. You can substitute brown lentils.*

POACHED EGGS WITH BACON, PEAS, MUSHROOMS, AND TRUFFLE OIL

Serves 4

2 tablespoons ½-inch pieces of smoked bacon (preferably Benton's)

4 large eggs

2 sprigs thyme

2 sprigs flat-leaf parsley

1 bay leaf

1 tablespoon white peppercorns

2 tablespoons plus 2 teaspoons olive oil

1 cup thinly sliced garlic (preferably young garlic)

2 cups vegetable stock

2 tablespoons crème fraîche

1 tablespoon lecithin (see Note)

Salt and freshly ground white pepper

¼ cup chanterelle mushrooms

2 cups petite peas, blanched

1 tablespoon thinly sliced fresh chives

1½ teaspoons fresh lemon thyme leaves

¼ teaspoon finely grated lemon zest

1 teaspoon freshly squeezed lemon juice

2 tablespoons duck jus or beef stock

1 tablespoon black truffle oil

Edible flowers (such as borage or marigolds; optional)

In a small skillet over medium heat, cook the bacon pieces until crispy, 8 to 10 minutes. Drain on paper towels and set aside.

To poach the eggs, fill a small saucepan with about 1 inch of water. Place it over high heat to boil it quickly, then decrease to a simmer. Stir the water clockwise with a spoon to create a swirling effect, then carefully crack an egg and gently slide it into the water so the yolk does not break. Gently spoon water over the egg so the white cooks quickly and covers the yolk. Cook for 1 to 2 minutes, until the white is firm but the yolk is still runny. Use a slotted spoon to gently transfer the egg to a small bowl.

Repeat with the remaining eggs, transferring them to separate bowls. Set aside.

To prepare the garlic sauce, combine the thyme, parsley, bay leaf, and white peppercorns in a square of cheesecloth and use kitchen twine to tie them up in a sachet. Heat 2 teaspoons of olive oil in a large skillet over medium heat, and cook the garlic until tender, about 10 minutes. Add the vegetable stock and the sachet and simmer for 20 minutes. Add the crème fraîche and lecithin.Remove the sachet and transfer the contents to a blender. Blend at high speed for 2 minutes to form a smooth puree. Pass the mixture through a chinois (fine-mesh sieve), taste, and adjust the seasoning with salt and white pepper. Transfer the mixture to a high-sided sauce-pot and set aside.

Heat the 2 tablespoons of olive oil in a medium sauté pan over medium heat and cook the mushrooms for 10 minutes, until soft. Add the reserved bacon and continue cooking another minute longer. Add the peas, chives, lemon thyme leaves, lemon zest, and lemon juice. Stir and cook another 3 minutes until heated through. Season with salt and white pepper to taste.

To serve, divide the pea and bacon mixture among 4 bowls. Make a hole in the center for the eggs. Use a spoon to carefully place an egg in the center of each bowl of the pea mixture. Spoon a little of the duck jus over each egg and around the peas. Use an immersion blender to foam the garlic sauce and spoon it over the pea mixture. Top each with truffle oil and flowers, and serve immediately.

NOTE: *Lecithin is sold as a food supplement and for medical uses. In cooking, it is often used as an emulsifier, especially for chocolate and candy.*

EGGS WITH VADOUVAN FINGERS AND BACON EMULSION

Serves 4

4 large eggs

2 tablespoons canola oil

6 large Trumpet Royale mushrooms, quartered, or 1 cup chanterelle mushrooms

Salt and freshly ground black pepper

1 teaspoon finely grated shallot (see Notes)

1 teaspoon finely grated garlic

½ teaspoon fresh thyme leaves

1 teaspoon soy sauce

1 teaspoon honey

½ cup chicken stock

2 teaspoons unsalted butter

1 teaspoon lemon oil

4 asparagus spears, peeled

½ cup vegetable stock

VADOUVAN FINGERS

2 teaspoons plus 2 tablespoons unsalted butter, at room temperature

1 slice Texas toast, cut vertically into 4 fingers, crusts discarded

1 tablespoon vadouvan spice (see Notes)

1 teaspoon Demerara sugar

BACON EMULSION

1 pound applewood-smoked bacon, diced

¼ cup diced Spanish onion

1 stalk celery, diced

1 carrot, diced

1 clove garlic, peeled

4 cups chicken stock

1 sprig thyme

1 teaspoon unsalted butter

2 teaspoons sherry vinegar

TO SERVE

Fleur de sel

Piment d'Espelette (see Notes) or paprika

Fresh chives

To prepare soft-boiled eggs, fill a small pot with enough water to cover the eggs and bring it to a boil. Add the eggs and cook for 6 minutes. Remove the pan from the heat, carefully drain off the water, and rinse the eggs under cool water. Refrigerate the eggs while you prepare the rest of the ingredients.

Heat the canola oil in a medium sauté pan over medium heat. When hot, add the mushrooms and season with salt and pepper. Cook until caramelized, 5 to 7 minutes. Add the shallot, grated garlic, thyme leaves, soy sauce, and honey. Continue cooking until there is no liquid left, 3 to 5 minutes. Add the ½ cup of chicken stock and 1 teaspoon of the butter. Increase the heat to high and cook, swirling the pan occasionally, until the sauce thickens. Remove from the heat, adjust the seasoning if necessary, and set aside.

Heat the lemon oil in a medium sauté pan over high heat to just before the smoking point when the oil ripples. Working quickly, add the asparagus, salt, and black pepper. Just when the asparagus begins to lightly brown on one side, add the vegetable stock and the remaining 1 teaspoon butter. Cover the pan and cook on high heat until the asparagus is tender and the sauce begins to thicken. Remove from the heat, adjust the seasoning if necessary, and set aside.

To make the vadouvan fingers, spread 2 teaspoons of the butter on all sides of the bread fingers. Mix together the vadouvan spice and Demerara sugar and roll the bread fingers in them, making sure to coat all sides well. Heat the remaining 2 tablespoons of butter in a small sauté pan over medium heat until foamy. Add the bread fingers and cook slowly until caramelized on each side, about 4 minutes total. Set aside.

To make the bacon emulsion, in a large skillet over medium heat, cook the diced bacon until brown and crispy. Drain the bacon in a chinois (fine-mesh sieve) set over a bowl. Reserve both the fat and the bacon.

In the same skillet in which you cooked the bacon, cook the onion, celery, carrot, and whole garlic over medium-high heat until lightly caramelized, about 10 minutes. Add the reserved bacon, the 4 cups of chicken stock, and the sprig of thyme. Simmer gently (without reducing too much) for up to 2 hours, or until fully flavored.

Transfer the sauce mixture to a blender, add the butter, vinegar, and a teaspoon of the reserved bacon fat and blend on high speed for 3 to 4 minutes.

Season with salt and pepper to taste. Strain the mixture through a fine-mesh sieve into a bowl. Set aside.

When ready to serve, gently warm all of the ingredients (or keep them warm in the oven throughout the process). Divide the mushroom mixture among 4 small bowls. Top each portion with asparagus. Carefully crack and peel the eggs. Gently place one egg on top of the asparagus in each bowl. Sprinkle with fleur de sel and Piment d'Espelette, and garnish with chives.

With an immersion blender, whip the bacon sauce until frothy. Spoon the sauce onto the eggs, place a vadouvan finger on top of each, and serve.

NOTES: *Vadouvan spice is an Indian spice mixture created by sautéing a curry spice blend in olive oil with onions, forming a curry paste. The spice mix includes curry leaves, fenugreek, mustard seeds, garlic, and sometimes cumin. As with most regional spices, there is no exact recipe, and the ingredients may vary. Most chefs make their own blend. Any curry blend will work mixed with sautéed onion in place of the vadouvan spice.*

Piment d'Espelette is a small red pepper from Espelette, France, often found in dried or powdered forms in America. It has a smoked paprika flavor and can be substituted with paprika.

EXECUTIVE CHEF CHRISTOPHER KRONNER, **BAR TARTINE, SAN FRANCISCO, CALIFORNIA**

SAVORY BACON BREAD PUDDING

Serves 4

6 ounces thick-cut bacon, cut into ½-inch pieces

6 ounces sharp cheddar cheese, cut into ½-inch cubes

¼ cup chopped fresh sage

5 cups torn day-old country bread

6 large eggs

2 cups whole milk

1 tablespoon salt

In a medium skillet over medium heat, cook the bacon pieces until crispy. Drain on paper towels and set aside.

Preheat the oven to 400°F.

Place the bacon, cheese, sage, and bread in a large bowl. In a separate large bowl, beat the eggs and add the milk to form a custard. Whisk in the salt. Pour the custard over the dry ingredients, mix thoroughly, and allow the mixture to sit for 15 minutes.

Pour the mixture into a 4 by 8-inch greased loaf pan and cover with aluminum foil. Place the loaf pan into a metal roasting pan and pour hot water into the roasting pan until it reaches three-quarters of the way up the sides of the loaf pan.

Bake for 45 minutes. Remove the foil and bake for 15 minutes longer to allow the top to brown and the pudding to rise. Cool for 20 minutes before removing from the pan, slicing, and serving.

NOTE: *This bread pudding is also good the next day cut into slices and reheated by frying in a skillet until brown on both sides.*

GARETH HUGHES, **DUB PIES, NEW YORK, NEW YORK**

BREAKFAST PIE

Makes 1 (9-inch) pie

9 slices bacon

1 (9-inch) prepared pie crust, defrosted if necessary

6 large eggs

2 cups grated cheddar cheese (8 ounces; preferably white Vermont cheddar)

1 sheet frozen puff pastry, thawed

Preheat the oven to 350°F.

In a medium skillet over medium heat, cook the bacon until crispy, about 10 minutes. Drain and cool on a rack or paper towels. Chop into small pieces.

Sprinkle the chopped bacon across the bottom of the pie crust, then break 5 of the eggs over the bacon. Top with the cheese. Moisten the edges of the pastry with water. Place the thawed puff pastry on top, cut it to fit, and press to seal the two crusts together. Cut slits in the top for steam to escape.

Mix the remaining egg in a small bowl with a little water, then brush the top of the pastry with the mixture. Bake until the pastry is golden, the cheese is melted, and the egg is cooked, about 30 minutes. Serve warm.

CHEF ELLEN BURKE VAN SLYKE, CREATIVE DIRECTOR OF FOOD AND BEVERAGE,
LOEWS CORONADO BAY RESORT AND SPA, SAN DIEGO, CALIFORNIA

BACON, ASPARAGUS, AND GRUYÈRE QUICHE

Serves 4 to 6

8 slices applewood-smoked bacon

6 asparagus spears

1 (9-inch) prepared pie crust

1¼ cups shredded Gruyère cheese (5 ounces)

5 large eggs

½ cup crème fraîche (see Note)

½ cup whole milk

½ cup half-and-half

Sea salt and freshly cracked black pepper (preferably Malabar)

In a large skillet over medium heat, cook the bacon until crispy. Drain on a rack or paper towels. Crumble and set aside.

In a wide saucepan, bring 1 inch of water to a boil over medium heat. Add the asparagus and boil for 3 to 4 minutes, being careful not to overcook. Immediately rinse the asparagus under cold water. Drain and cut into ½-inch pieces.

Preheat the oven to 375°F.

Line a 9-inch pie pan with the pie crust. Distribute the crumbled bacon and asparagus evenly across the bottom. Spread the shredded cheese on top. In a large bowl, whisk the eggs until creamy yellow. Add the crème fraîche, milk, and half-and-half, and season with salt and pepper. Pour the egg mixture over the bacon, asparagus, and cheese.

Bake for 30 minutes, or until the egg mixture is fully cooked and the top is golden. Serve warm.

NOTE: *To make your own crème fraîche, whisk together equal parts sour cream and heavy whipping cream. Cover and let stand overnight at room temperature. Refrigerate in the morning.*

MEDITERRANEAN BLTS

Serves 4

FOCACCIA

2 cups warm water

1 tablespoon active bread yeast

¼ cup extra-virgin olive oil, plus more for drizzling

5 cups all-purpose flour, plus more as needed

Kosher salt

Fresh rosemary, or olives, or thinly sliced green onions, or other topping of choice (optional; see Note)

ROASTED RED PEPPER AÏOLI

1 red bell pepper

⅓ cup plus 1 tablespoon extra-virgin olive oil

1 egg yolk

1 teaspoon Dijon mustard

2 cloves garlic, peeled

1 teaspoon freshly squeezed lemon juice

Pinch of kosher salt

TO ASSEMBLE

16 thick slices smoked bacon (see Note)

½ pound salad greens (preferably a mix including Lolla Rosa and baby arugula)

2 large tomatoes (preferably heirloom, Jersey, or beefsteak), sliced

To make the focaccia, add the warm water to a medium bowl, dissolve the yeast in it, and let the mixture proof in a warm area for 10 minutes. Add ¼ cup of the olive oil and stir.

Mix the flour and salt in the bowl of an electric mixer fitted with a dough hook. Slowly add the yeast mixture while running the mixer on low speed. Increase the speed to medium and mix until the dough is smooth and pulling away from the sides of the bowl. If the dough is too moist, add a little more flour, a little bit at a time, until the dough comes together and pulls away from the sides.

Oil a baking sheet and stretch the dough to fit the pan. Brush the dough with olive oil, and sprinkle with kosher salt and the toppings, if desired. Cover with plastic wrap and leave in a warm spot to rise for about 1 hour until doubled.

Preheat the oven to 375°F. Remove the plastic and lightly dimple the dough with your fingers. Drizzle with more olive oil. Bake for 15 to 20 minutes, until golden brown. Transfer the baking sheet to a rack.

To prepare the roasted red pepper aïoli, roast the bell pepper over the flame on a gas stovetop or barbecue grill. Keep turning it, allowing all sides to char. Once it is well charred, place the pepper in a bowl, cover with plastic wrap, and allow to cool. When completely cooled, peel off the skin. Remove and discard the core and seeds. Puree the flesh with 1 tablespoon of the olive oil in a food processor. Set aside.

Clean the food processor bowl, then puree the egg yolk, Dijon mustard, and garlic until smooth. Add the lemon juice and briefly pulse. With the processor running, slowly add the remaining ⅓ cup olive oil in a very thin stream. The mixture will emulsify into a mayonnaise, or aïoli. Fold in the pureed pepper.

In a large skillet over medium heat, cook the bacon until crispy. Drain on a rack or paper towels. Set aside.

Divide the focaccia into 4 rectangles. Slice each piece horizontally into a top and bottom half. Spread each of the halves generously with the aioli and arrange them aioli side up on a baking sheet. Top each of the 4 bottom slices of bread with 4 slices of bacon.

Place the baking sheet in a warm (200°F) oven to warm through, about 5 minutes.

Remove the baking sheet from the oven, place a handful of greens on top of the bacon, followed by slices of tomato. Place the tops on the sandwiches and cut each in half to serve.

NOTE: *Chef Byrne loves to use rosemary or green onion focaccia, and she prefers bacon from Faicco's Italian Specialties in New York City.*

SMALL BITES

Bacon-Wrapped Mango Chutney-and
Manchego-Stuffed Dates 26

Bacon-Wrapped Parmigiano-Stuffed Dates 28

Patatas Bravas 29

Adulterated Accordion Potatoes 30

Bacon and Tuna Poke 33

Bacon Hash on Crostini 34

Cocktail BLTs 35

Roasted Oysters with Bacon Crumbs 36

Kobe Beef and Bacon Sliders 38

BACON-WRAPPED MANGO CHUTNEY– AND MANCHEGO-STUFFED DATES

Makes 12, serves 6

12 large Medjool dates (see Note)

1 cup mango chutney

1 cup grated manchego cheese (4 ounces)

6 slices applewood-smoked bacon

Preheat the oven to 350°F. Line a baking sheet with parchment paper.

Use a paring knife to cut each date in half lengthwise just to the pit. Remove the pit and open the date, but do not cut all the way through it.

In a small bowl, combine the chutney and cheese with a small fork, mashing it together lightly. Spoon a teaspoon of the filling into the center of each date. Close the date around the filling.

Cut each of the bacon slices in half. Wrap a half piece of bacon tightly around the center of each date. Place the dates on the baking sheet. Bake for 8 to 10 minutes, until the bacon is crispy. Drain the bacon on paper towels. Spear each with a toothpick to serve.

NOTE: *Medjool dates are some of the best in the world. Originally from Morocco, the Medjool date was traditionally reserved for royal hosts and other dignitaries. Prepared this way as "devils on horseback" they are one of the most popular starters in Chef Allen's restaurant.*

BACON-WRAPPED PARMIGIANO-STUFFED DATES

Makes 12, serves 6

12 Medjool dates (see Notes)

½ pound Parmigiano-Reggiano cheese (whole, not grated)

12 slices thick bacon (see Notes)

Preheat the oven to 350°F. Line a baking sheet with parchment paper.

Pit the dates if necessary. It will be pretty easy if you begin at the stem end and pull. The pits are attached to the stem end and should pull out fairly easily. Cut the cheese into little batons about ¼ inch thick and the length of the dates, reserving some for garnishing later. Stuff each date with one baton. Wrap each date in 1 bacon strip.

Place the bacon-wrapped dates on the baking sheet with the bacon end down. Roast for 15 to 20 minutes, until golden brown and crispy. Drain briefly on paper towels and serve warm, topped with freshly grated Parmigiano-Reggiano.

NOTES: *The bigger and fresher the dates, the better. Chef Byrne also recommends using good-quality bacon. She uses thick, double-smoked bacon.*

These sweet and savory bites go beautifully with a glass of sparkling wine and are a terrific treat for special occasions, such as New Year's Eve. These are delicious but decadent, so two per person is usually a good serving size.

EXECUTIVE CHEF MICHELLE BERNSTEIN, **SRA. MARTINEZ, MIAMI, FLORIDA**

PATATAS BRAVAS

Makes 50, serves 20 to 30

50 tiny Red Bliss, creamer, or fingerling potatoes

¼ cup olive oil

Salt and freshly ground black pepper

Grapeseed oil or canola oil, for frying

25 slices pancetta, halved

¼ cup canola oil

3 shallots, chopped

2 cloves garlic, minced

1 tablespoon aji amarillo paste (see Note)

1 (8-ounce) package cream cheese, at room temperature

5 saltine crackers

1 (14.5-ounce) can evaporated milk

Juice of 1 lime

50 cilantro leaves, kept cold until use

Preheat the oven to 425F°.

Toss the potatoes in a large bowl with the olive oil, then season with salt and pepper. Place the potatoes on a roasting rack set over a baking pan; wrap the pan setup completely in aluminum foil. Bake until tender, 20 to 25 minutes. Cool completely. If the potatoes are very small, slice ¼ inch off the top and the bottom so that they stand up straight; if the potatoes are long fingerlings, cut them in half first before you slice off each end. Using a small melon baller or espresso spoon, scoop out the insides of the potatoes, leaving about ½ inch of the bottom intact.

Pour enough grapeseed oil into a frying pan to reach about halfway up the sides of the pan and heat to 350°F. In small batches, fry the pancetta, making sure you place each piece in the oil one at a time and cook until they stop bubbling. Remove them in batches and drain on paper towels. (You can cook the pancetta a few hours ahead of time and leave it at room temperature until you're ready to use it.) Using the same oil in which you fried the pancetta, cook the potatoes in small batches of about 5 at a time, for about 2 minutes per batch, or until golden brown. Drain on paper towels.

Heat the ¼ cup of canola oil in a sauté pan over low heat, add the shallots and garlic, and cook until soft and translucent, about 5 minutes. Transfer them to a blender, add the aji amarillo paste, cream cheese, crackers, and evaporated milk, and puree until very smooth. Add the lime juice and season with salt.

For best results, fill the fried potatoes using a squeeze bottle or espresso spoon. Fill each potato with a spoonful of sauce, top with a piece of crispy pancetta and a cilantro leaf, and serve.

NOTE: *Aji amarillo paste is made from the chile pepper of the same name and is available in the grocery store. Check the Latin foods aisle.*

EXECUTIVE CHEF MICAH EDELSTEIN, **THE WANDERING CHEF; GRASS RESTAURANT & LOUNGE, MIAMI, FLORIDA**

ADULTERATED ACCORDION POTATOES

Makes 18, serves 6 to 8

2 cups raw, shelled pumpkin seeds (see Note)

¼ cup extra-virgin olive oil, plus more as needed

Kosher salt and freshly ground black pepper

2 teaspoons garam masala (see Note)

1 tablespoon chili powder

¼ pound pancetta or regular bacon, diced (see Notes)

18 new Red Bliss or Yukon gold potatoes, skin on

1 tablespoon fresh thyme leaves, chopped, or ½ teaspoon dried thyme

3 cloves garlic, minced

⅓ cup crumbled blue cheese (3 ounces)

1 tablespoon Greek yogurt, plus more if desired (see Notes)

Preheat the oven to 375°F. Fill a large bowl with ice water.

Toss the pumpkin seeds in a medium bowl with 1 tablespoon of olive oil, the salt, pepper, and the garam masala and chili powder, then roast on a baking sheet until golden and fragrant, about 10 minutes. Cool. Leave the oven on. (You can make these a day ahead and store in an airtight container, if desired.)

In a medium skillet over medium heat, cook the pancetta until it crisps, about 5 minutes. Drain on paper towels and blot with a brown paper bag to remove as much of the rendered fat as possible. Set aside.

Use a melon baller to scoop a small "bowl" out of the center of each potato. Make sure the potatoes all sit steadily on a flat surface, bowl side up. If any are wobbly, cut a small slice off of the bottom side. Use a paring knife to make cuts every ¼ inch or so straight across each potato. The cuts should go about three-quarters of the way through each potato. Be careful not to cut all the way through, so the potato stays together. The potatoes should look like accordions with hollow middles. Submerge the potatoes in the ice water as you finish cutting them so they do not turn brown.

Pat the potatoes dry and toss them in a large bowl with 3 tablespoons of olive oil, salt, pepper, thyme, and garlic, adding more olive oil if necessary. Spread the potatoes evenly on a baking sheet and bake until deep golden brown and crunchy, about 20 minutes. Depending on your oven, you may have to broil them briefly at the end to crisp them properly. Remove the potatoes from the oven but leave the oven on.

In a bowl or food processor, blend together the blue cheese and Greek yogurt until smooth and creamy. You can add more yogurt to taste to cut the bite of the blue cheese.

To serve, while the potatoes are still warm fill each potato "bowl" with the blue cheese mixture, then top with pancetta bits and spiced pumpkin seeds. Serve warm.

NOTES: *The pumpkin seeds are great to use in salads or as a snack, so you may want to make a larger batch than is necessary for the potatoes.*

Garam masala is a basic blend of ground spices common in Indian and other South Asian cuisines. The word garam *refers to spice intensity, not heat; garam masala is pungent, but not "hot" in the same way as a chile pepper.*

Pancetta is an Italian bacon cured with salt and spices but not smoked. It is flavorful and slightly salty, and it comes in a large sausage-like roll, unlike the bacon most Americans are familiar with. You can find it at Italian delis and gourmet markets, and it can usually be substituted as such in any recipe that calls for traditional American bacon.

Greek yogurt is a thick yogurt available in many grocery stores and specialty markets. If you cannot find it, you may substitute regular (not nonfat) yogurt.

BACON AND TUNA POKE

Makes 18, serves 4 to 6

SOY-SESAME DRESSING

¼ cup low-sodium soy sauce

2 tablespoons sesame oil

2 tablespoons water

1 teaspoon crushed red chili flakes

1 teaspoon salt

1 teaspoon cracked black pepper

1 tablespoon sesame seeds, toasted

1 pound thick-cut smoked bacon, diced

2 pounds yellowfin tuna, diced into ¼-inch pieces

½ cup finely diced red onion

1 tablespoon minced fresh ginger

1 tablespoon minced garlic

½ cup chopped green onions

TO SERVE

2 avocados, pitted, peeled, and mashed into a pulp

18 fried wonton wrappers

To make the dressing, in a medium bowl, combine the soy sauce, sesame oil, water, chili flakes, salt, pepper, and sesame seeds and whisk well. Set aside.

In a large skillet over medium-low heat, slowly cook the diced bacon, stirring continuously, until it is about 50 percent rendered. Drain on paper towels. (Chef Aglibot likes the bacon cubes to be tender, not crispy, but if you like crispy, make them crispy.)

In a large bowl, combine the bacon, tuna, onion, ginger, garlic, and green onions. Add the dressing and toss to combine. Season with salt and pepper to taste.

To serve, spoon 1 tablespoon of mashed avocado on top of each fried wonton wrapper, and then top with 1 tablespoon of the bacon-tuna mixture.

NOTE: *Tuna poke is a Hawaiian raw tuna salad similar in style to steak tartare. Keep the tuna refrigerated until you're ready to mix it in.*

CHEF PHILIPPE TROSCH, **SOFITEL HOTEL, PHILADELPHIA, PENNSYLVANIA**

BACON HASH ON CROSTINI

Serves 6

½ pound bacon, cut into large pieces (about 1 cup)

¼ cup shredded or diced yellow onion

1 tablespoon unsalted butter

3 tablespoons dark brown sugar

2 large russet potatoes, peeled and shredded

Salt and freshly ground black pepper, or Piment d'Espelette, or cayenne pepper

1 loaf of bread of your choice (such as baguette)

In a heavy sauté pan over medium heat, cook the bacon until crispy, about 10 minutes. Add the onion and butter and cook, scraping the bits from the bottom of the pan, until the onion is dark golden, about 10 minutes. Add the brown sugar and shredded potato; stir to coat. Cook the mixture until thick and almost dry, about 10 minutes. Watch carefully to ensure that it doesn't burn. Season with salt and pepper to taste.

Slice the bread and toast it to your liking. To serve, spread a spoonful of hash on top of the toast pieces.

NOTE: *This makes a great cocktail snack and is also good as an appetizer served with a green salad.*

CHEF ELLEN BURKE VAN SLYKE, CREATIVE DIRECTOR OF FOOD AND BEVERAGE,
LOEWS CORONADO BAY RESORT AND SPA, SAN DIEGO, CALIFORNIA

COCKTAIL BLTS

Makes 16, serves 4 to 8

MEYER LEMON AÏOLI

1 egg yolk

½ teaspoon Dijon mustard

Juice and grated zest of 1 Meyer lemon

Sea salt and freshly cracked black pepper

1 cup extra-virgin olive oil

8 slices thick-cut applewood-smoked bacon

8 slices brioche bread

16 sun-dried tomatoes

8 large butter lettuce leaves

To make the lemon aïoli, combine the egg yolk, mustard, lemon juice, and salt and pepper to taste in a medium bowl or in the bowl of a food processor. Whisk or pulse until the mixture is yellow and frothy. Slowly drizzle in the olive oil, whisking or pulsing until completely emulsified. Add the lemon zest and whisk or pulse. Refrigerate until ready to use.

Lay the bacon slices in a large skillet over medium heat and cook to your desired degree of doneness. Drain on a rack or paper towels. Toast the brioche slices. Spread the aïoli on each piece of toast. Top 4 of the pieces of toast each with 4 sun-dried tomatoes, 2 bacon slices, and 2 lettuce leaves. Top the bottom halves with the top pieces of toast. Cut the sandwiches into quarters and serve.

CHEF/OWNER RICK TRAMONTO, TRU, CHICAGO, ILLINOIS

ROASTED OYSTERS WITH BACON CRUMBS

Makes 12, serves 2 to 6

8 slices thick-cut bacon

8 tablespoons (1 stick) unsalted butter, at room temperature

3 cloves garlic, minced

⅓ cup coarsely chopped shallots

⅓ cup coarsely chopped red bell pepper

½ cup coarsely chopped celery, with leaves

Juice and zest of ½ lemon, plus ½ lemon, quartered

2 sprigs oregano, leaves removed, stems discarded

2 sprigs thyme, leaves only

¼ teaspoon crushed red chili flakes

½ cup panko (Japanese breadcrumbs)

¼ cup grated Parmigiano-Reggiano cheese

Kosher salt and freshly ground black pepper

12 large oysters on the half shell

SEASONED ROCK SALT

6 cups rock salt

¼ cup star anise

¼ cup pink peppercorns

¼ cup black peppercorns

3 cinnamon sticks, broken into 2 to 3 pieces each

⅓ bunch flat-leaf parsley, finely chopped, for garnish

Preheat the oven to 425°F. Line a baking sheet with parchment paper.

Lay the bacon in a single layer on the baking sheet and bake for 10 to 12 minutes, until crispy. Leave the oven on, and reserve the bacon fat from the baking sheet.

Place the butter, garlic, shallots, bell pepper, celery, lemon zest and juice, oregano, thyme, and chili flakes in a food processor; pulse until the mixture is well combined but still has texture. Add the panko and cheese and pulse to incorporate them into the mixture. Transfer the mixture to a large bowl.

Crumble the bacon into large chunks, set aside 2 tablespoons, and add the rest of it to the mixture.

Drizzle the mixture with the reserved bacon fat and stir. Season with salt and black pepper to taste.

Open the oysters and separate the shell from the muscle. Lay out the oysters in their half shells in a single layer on a baking sheet. Place about 1 tablespoon of the breadcrumb-bacon mixture on top of each oyster. Place on a baking pan and bake until bubbly, 10 to 12 minutes.

To make the seasoned rock salt, in a large mixing bowl, combine the salt with the star anise, peppercorns, and cinnamon sticks. Place the rock salt mixture on a large platter and arrange the oysters on top for stability. Top with the parsley, the reserved chopped bacon, and the lemon wedges, and serve.

KOBE BEEF AND BACON SLIDERS

Makes 2

ROASTED GARLIC AÏOLI

1 tablespoon egg yolk

1 large clove roasted garlic (see Notes)

1 teaspoon Dijon mustard

2 tablespoons freshly squeezed lime juice

½ cup grapeseed oil

½ teaspoon chopped fresh flat-leaf parsley

½ teaspoon chopped fresh basil

½ teaspoon sriracha hot sauce, or hot sauce of your choice

½ teaspoon southwest seasoning salt, or to taste (see Notes)

BURGERS

4 slices applewood-smoked bacon

2 (3-ounce) Kobe beef burger patties, 3 inches wide and ½ inch thick (see Notes)

Kosher salt and freshly cracked black pepper

2 thin slices white cheddar cheese

2 brioche buns (see Notes)

Olive oil, for the buns

To make the roasted garlic aïoli, place the egg yolk, garlic, mustard, and lime juice in a food processor; with the machine running, slowly incorporate the grapeseed oil until the mixture emulsifies into a mayonnaise. Transfer the mixture to a bowl and use a spatula to fold in the basil, parsley, and sriracha sauce. Add the southwest seasoning salt. Set aside.

Preheat the oven to 375°F. Prepare a grill to cook over direct high heat.

Cook the bacon in a large skillet over medium heat until crispy, or lay the pieces on a baking sheet and bake for 15 minutes, until crispy. Drain on paper towels and set aside. Leave the oven on.

Season the burger patties with salt and black pepper, then place them on the grill and grill to rare doneness, 2 to 3 minutes per side (or your preferred doneness).

To serve, top each burger patty with 2 slices of bacon, followed by a slice of cheese. Transfer the patties to a sizzle plate or baking pan and heat in the oven under the broiler until the cheese melts.

Slice the brioche buns in half, brush with olive oil, and toast them lightly on the grill. Spread a generous amount of roasted garlic aïoli on each side of each bun, then assemble the burgers. Serve immediately.

NOTES: *Chef Brasel serves sliders two ways: on a brioche bun with mango mustard, foie gras, and caramelized onions; or on a brioche bun with applewood-smoked bacon, New York white cheddar cheese, and roasted garlic aïoli.*

You can roast a whole head of garlic and use it in many ways. It should keep in the refrigerator for up to a week. Before roasting, remove loose pieces of the skins and cut the tips of the head off so the garlic pieces are exposed a little. Drizzle with 1 tablespoon of extra-virgin olive oil, making sure the whole head is oiled well. Place in a muffin pan, cover with aluminum foil, and roast at 350°F for 30 minutes.

Several southwest seasoning salts (such as Lawry's) are available in supermarkets across the country. This is usually a blend of chili powder, paprika, cumin, coriander, cayenne, oregano, garlic powder, red chili flakes, salt, and black pepper.

If you can't find ground Kobe beef, use fatty top chuck ground beef.

Brioche is a dense egg- and butter-based bread available at many grocery stores and gourmet markets.

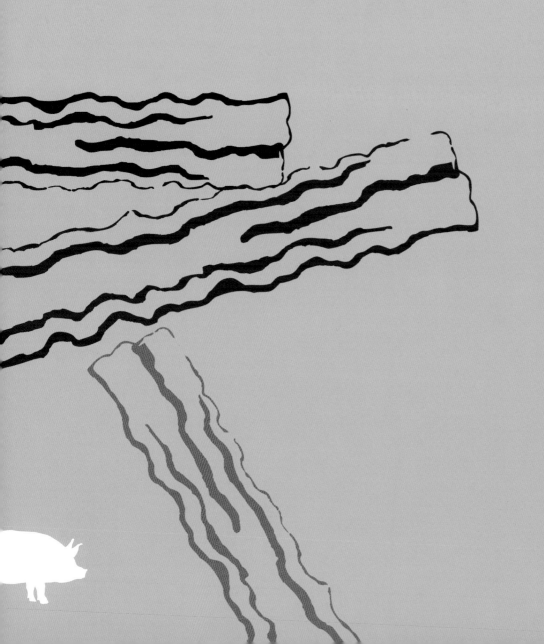

SOUPS, SALADS, AND SIDES

Egg Chowder with Bacon and New Potatoes 43

Roasted Tomato and Smoked Bacon Bisque 45

Spicy Braised Bacon with Spagna Beans
and Treviso Radicchio 47

Grilled Bacon and Cucumber Salad
with Chili Caramel Dressing 49

Braised Artichokes with Bacon
and Black Trumpet Mushrooms 50

Bacon-Pineapple Fried Orzo 51

EGG CHOWDER WITH BACON AND NEW POTATOES

Serves 5 to 6

6 large eggs

¼ cup distilled white vinegar

½ pound thick-cut bacon

4 tablespoons (½ stick) unsalted butter

1 medium onion, cut into ¾-inch dice

1 teaspoon fresh thyme leaves (from 2 to 3 sprigs), chopped

1 teaspoon dry English mustard (preferably Colman's)

1½ pounds red or white new potatoes, halved and sliced ⅓-inch thick

3 cups chicken stock

1 cup heavy whipping cream

Kosher or sea salt and freshly ground black pepper

2 tablespoons chopped fresh chives, for garnish

Place the eggs in a 1½- to 2-quart saucepan and add the vinegar and enough water to completely cover them. Bring to a boil, then lower the heat and cook the eggs at a steady simmer for 5 minutes. Remove the eggs from the heat and let them sit in the water for 10 minutes.

Rinse the eggs under cold running water until cool enough to handle, then peel them. Cut 5 of the eggs into medium dice as follows: quarter them lengthwise, then cut each quarter into 3 to 4 pieces. Cover and leave at room temperature to add to the chowder later. Chop the remaining egg into ⅓-inch dice and refrigerate for use as a garnish, removing it from the refrigerator about 15 minutes before you serve the chowder.

In a 10- to 12-inch sauté pan, gently fry the slices of bacon, in batches, over medium-low heat, until crisp and golden brown. Drain on paper towels. Pour off all except 1 tablespoon of the fat from the pan, and set the pan aside. Cut the bacon into large pieces about 1 inch wide. Place in an ovenproof dish, cover, and reserve.

Return the pan to the stove and turn the heat to medium. Add the butter, onion, and thyme and sauté, stirring occasionally with a wooden spoon, for 6 to 8 minutes, until the onion is softened but not browned. Stir in the dry mustard and cook for 1 minute more.

Add the potatoes and stock. The stock should just barely cover the potatoes; if it doesn't, add enough water to cover them. Bring to a simmer over medium heat and simmer for 10 to 12 minutes, until the potatoes are fully cooked and tender.

Remove the pan from the heat, stir in the 5 medium-dice eggs and the cream, and season to taste with salt and black pepper. If you are not serving the chowder within the hour, let it cool a bit and refrigerate; cover the chowder after it has chilled completely. Otherwise let it sit at room temperature for up to an hour, allowing the egg flavor to blend with the broth.

When ready to serve, reheat the chowder over low heat, but don't let it boil. Even though the eggs are hard boiled, the yolks will lightly thicken the chowder. Warm the bacon in a low oven (200°F) for a few minutes.

Using a slotted spoon, mound the onion, potatoes, and eggs in the center of large plates or bowls, then ladle the broth around. Scatter the bacon over individual servings and sprinkle with the reserved diced egg and the chives.

NOTE: *This recipe is too humble for entertaining and too filling to serve as a starter, but it makes a nice family dish for lunch or supper. Serve with crackers or biscuits. This recipe was first published in Chef White's* 50 Chowders *(Scribner, 2000), the first hardcover cookbook to explore the many interpretations of chowders.*

ROASTED TOMATO AND SMOKED BACON BISQUE

Serves 4 to 6

5 pounds vine-ripened tomatoes

3 shallots, sliced, plus 2 shallots, minced

4 cloves garlic, minced, plus 8 cloves garlic, peeled whole

¼ cup plus 2 tablespoons extra-virgin olive oil

1 cup chopped applewood-smoked bacon

2 tablespoons unsalted butter

2 tablespoons vegetable oil

2 medium onions, coarsely chopped

2 stalks celery, coarsely chopped

3 carrots, coarsely chopped

Salt and freshly ground white pepper

1 bay leaf

1 small bunch thyme, stems removed

3¼ cups vegetable stock

3 cups heavy whipping cream

2 cups breadcrumbs (see Note)

1 cup grated aged manchego cheese (4 ounces) or cubed fresh mozzarella cheese

1 pint red and yellow teardrop tomatoes, cut in half lengthwise

Small bunch basil leaves, cut into chiffonade

Juice of 2 lemons

4 to 6 whole basil leaves, or basil oil, for garnish

Preheat the oven to 400°F.

Cut the tomatoes in half and gently remove all or most of the seeds. Toss them in a large bowl with the sliced shallots, minced garlic, and ¼ cup of the olive oil. Transfer the mixture to a baking sheet with the tomatoes skin side up, making sure all of the shallots, garlic, and olive oil are poured on top of the tomatoes. Bake for 10 to 12 minutes, until the skins start to brown and blister. Set the pan aside to cool. Once cool, remove the tomato skins.

In a large soup pot over medium heat, cook the bacon until browned, 8 to 10 minutes. Pour off the rendered fat. Add the butter, vegetable oil, onions, celery, carrots, minced shallots, and whole garlic cloves to the bacon in the pot. Season the mixture with salt and white pepper. Cook for about 15 minutes, until the vegetables are tender. Add the roasted tomatoes, bay leaf, thyme, and vegetable stock. Bring to a boil, then add the heavy cream. Simmer for 30 minutes.

Puree the soup in a blender in batches, then strain it through a fine-mesh sieve back into the soup pot. Season with salt and white pepper to taste.

In a large bowl, toss together the breadcrumbs, cheese, teardrop tomatoes, basil chiffonade, the remaining 2 tablespoons of olive oil, the lemon juice, and salt and white pepper to taste. Spoon the hot soup into bowls, then top with the breadcrumb mixture and garnish with a basil leaf or a drizzle of basil oil and serve.

NOTE: *You can make your own breadcrumbs by cutting a baguette into ¼-inch cubes, tossing the cubes with olive oil, seasoning with salt and black pepper, and toasting them on a baking sheet in a 375°F oven for about 15 minutes. Allow the croutons to cool, and then crumble them.*

EXECUTIVE CHEF CHRIS COSENTINO, **INCANTO**, **SAN FRANCISCO**, **CALIFORNIA**

SPICY BRAISED BACON WITH SPAGNA BEANS AND TREVISO RADICCHIO

Serves 6

2 cups Spagna beans or cannellini beans (see Notes)

1 head garlic, split, plus 8 cloves garlic, sliced

1 carrot

1 stalk celery

1 russet potato, peeled

Salt and freshly ground black pepper

3 tablespoons extra-virgin olive oil, plus more for drizzling

2 heads Treviso radicchio, sliced (see Notes)

12 slices Spicy Braised Bacon plus some of the braising liquid (page 4)

Cooking the beans is a 2-day process. Soak the beans in enough water to cover them overnight in the refrigerator. The next day, strain and rinse the beans. Place them in a pot large enough to cover with 6 cups of water and add the split head of garlic, the carrot, celery, and potato. The peeled potato will soften the skin on the beans so that they don't burst when they are cooking. Cook over low heat for about 2 hours, until tender. Remove from the heat, then remove the vegetables and discard them. Season the beans with salt and black pepper and a drizzle of olive oil.

Transfer the beans to a clean pot and slowly warm them over medium-low heat. Heat the 3 tablespoons olive oil in a large sauté pan over medium heat and add the sliced garlic. Once the garlic becomes aromatic, add the radicchio. Cook until wilted, stirring occasionally, 8 to 10 minutes.

Divide the beans among 6 warm bowls, then place several slices of the braised bacon in each bowl and spoon some warm braising liquid over the top. Drape the radicchio over the bacon, drizzle olive oil on top, and serve.

NOTES: *Spagna beans are Italian beans with long, green, slightly curved broad pods containing 5 to 6 large white beans. They are sometimes called butter beans. The Spagna beans here require two days of preparation, so be sure to plan ahead. You can use cannellini beans if Spagna beans are hard to find.*

Treviso is one type of radicchio. It is red in color, with an elongated shape similar to endive, and it has a slightly bitter flavor. You may substitute it with any radicchio available in your market.

CHEF CHRISTOPHER RENDELL, **DOUBLE CROWN, NEW YORK, NEW YORK**

GRILLED BACON AND CUCUMBER SALAD WITH CHILI CARAMEL DRESSING

Serves 4

CHILI CARAMEL DRESSING

2 cups sugar

2 cups water

4 large fresh red chiles, finely sliced into rounds, with seeds

3 tablespoons freshly squeezed lime juice

3 tablespoons nam pla (fish sauce)

¼ cup finely minced cilantro leaves

SALAD

12 (2 inch wide) slices Classic Cured Bacon (page 3)

1 large cucumber

2 cups fresh mint leaves

2 cups fresh cilantro leaves

1 bunch of approximately 5 green onions, finely sliced

2 tablespoons crispy garlic (see Note)

To make the dressing, in a heavy-bottomed pot, bring the sugar and water to a boil. Reduce the heat and simmer until the mixture turns into a golden caramel, about 15 minutes, stirring often.

In a small bowl, combine the chiles, lime juice, and fish sauce. Add them to the caramel and simmer for a few minutes to dissolve the caramel. Remove the pot from the heat and add the cilantro leaves. Allow the mixture to cool, but do not refrigerate.

Slice the bacon strips into 2-inch-long pieces. Place on a hot grill or griddle and cook on both sides for 1 to 2 minutes, until golden and crispy.

Drain on a rack or paper towels. Slice the cucumber in half lengthwise, remove the seeds, and slice each half into 4 equal parts. Then cut each part into 2-inch sticks. In a bowl, combine the cucumber, mint, cilantro, green onions, and crispy bacon. Dress the salad with the chili caramel dressing and divide it among 4 bowls. Sprinkle each salad with crispy garlic and serve.

NOTE: *You can make your own crispy garlic by frying it in a sauté pan, or you can purchase it at any Asian grocery store.*

EXECUTIVE CHEF JASON BERTHOLD, **RN74, SAN FRANCISCO, CALIFORNIA**

BRAISED ARTICHOKES WITH BACON AND BLACK TRUMPET MUSHROOMS

Serves 2 to 4

8 large artichokes

Juice of 4 lemons

2 tablespoons olive oil

6 ounces applewood-smoked slab bacon, cut into ½-inch pieces

4 shallots, sliced

2 carrots, cut into ¼-inch slices

5 cloves garlic, minced

2 sprigs thyme

2 bay leaves

Pinch of saffron threads

1 cup white wine

2 cups chicken or vegetable stock

¼ pound black trumpet mushrooms

2 tablespoons unsalted butter

2 tablespoons chopped fresh flat-leaf parsley

To clean the artichokes, fill a large bowl with 4 quarts of cold water and add the lemon juice. Peel off the outer leaves of the artichokes and use a paring knife to trim the base of the stem. Cut around the outside of the artichoke near the base. Continue trimming the base to remove all of the hard green outer parts. Slice along the pointed top of the artichoke, exposing the choke about ¼ inch above the top of the base. Use a tablespoon to scoop out the fuzzy choke, and place the cleaned artichoke heart into the lemon water. Depending on how quickly you work with the artichokes, they may begin to oxidize. This will be less noticeable once they are cooked.

Heat the olive oil in a wide sauté pan over low heat. Add the bacon pieces and cook until the fat begins to render. Add the shallots, carrots, garlic, thyme, bay leaves, and saffron. Continue cooking on low heat for 5 to 10 minutes to soften the ingredients, but don't let them caramelize.

Add the cleaned artichokes and increase the heat to medium. Stir in the white wine and simmer for 2 to 3 minutes. Add the chicken stock and mushrooms and simmer gently until the artichokes are tender, about 30 minutes.

Remove the artichokes from the pan and set them aside. Increase the heat to medium-high and simmer the liquid until it is reduced by two-thirds. Add the butter and parsley and reduce for 5 more minutes. Remove the sauce from the heat and let it rest for 5 minutes, then pour it over the artichokes and serve.

NOTE: *This dish is great with grilled fish, roasted pork or lamb, rice or barley pilaf, or boiled potatoes.*

BACON-PINEAPPLE FRIED ORZO

Serves 4

5 slices bacon

Canola oil

1 tablespoon minced garlic

1 tablespoon minced fresh ginger

½ cup sliced scallions, some green parts reserved for garnish

1 cup ¼-inch diced fresh pineapple

5 cups cooked orzo

3 tablespoons ponzu (preferably Wan Ja Shan organic) (see Note)

Kosher salt and freshly ground black pepper

Cook the bacon in a large sauté pan or wok over medium heat until crispy. Drain the bacon on paper towels or a rack and set it aside. Drain the fat from the pan, wipe the pan clean, and lightly coat it with canola oil. Over medium heat, sauté the garlic, ginger, scallions, and pineapple until softened. Line up the bacon strips and coarsely chop with a knife. Add the cooked orzo, ponzu, and bacon. Toss to combine and heat through. Check the flavoring and season with salt and black pepper to taste. Serve family style, garnished with the reserved scallion greens.

NOTE: *Ponzu is a special Japanese sauce found at most Asian markets and some supermarkets.*

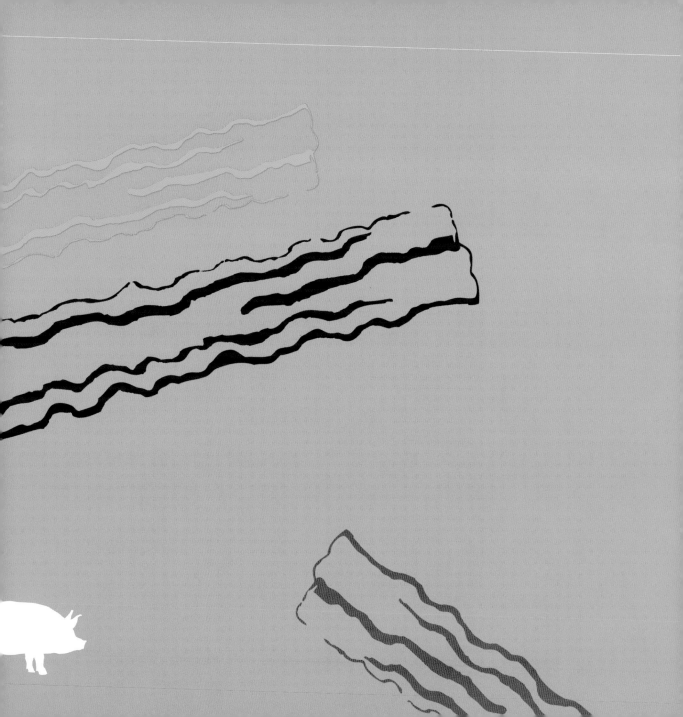

PASTA

Crispy Pork Belly Stir-Fry with Rice Noodles,
Green Peppercorns, and Thai Basil 54

Spaghetti Carbonara 56

Bucatini with Amatriciana Sauce 57

Bacon Mac and Cheese 59

Pasta with Brussels Sprouts, Cauliflower
Hazelnuts, and Bacon 60

Fall Risotto with Roasted Butternut Squash
and Double-Smoked Bacon 61

CHEF/OWNER IAN CHALERMKITTICHAI, **CUISINE CONCEPT CO., LTD., BANGKOK, THAILAND**

CRISPY PORK BELLY STIR-FRY WITH RICE NOODLES, GREEN PEPPERCORNS, AND THAI BASIL

Serves 6

5 tablespoons canola oil

2 long red fresh chile peppers, finely chopped

5 cloves garlic, chopped

¼ cup thinly sliced lesser ginger or fresh ginger (see Notes)

½ cup Thai basil, plus more for serving (see Notes)

2 tablespoons nam pla (fish sauce)

2 tablespoons oyster sauce

¼ cup coconut milk

5 tablespoons chicken stock

3 sprigs fresh green peppercorn or 1 tablespoon green peppercorns in brine (see Notes)

½ teaspoon superfine sugar

1 pound dried rice noodles, soaked in cold water for 30 minutes

12 slices Crispy Pork Belly (page 6), cut into 1-inch pieces

Heat the oil in a wok over low heat. Add the chiles and garlic and cook, stirring slowly, until they become fragrant, about 5 minutes. Add the ginger, the ½ cup of basil, the fish sauce, oyster sauce, coconut milk, chicken stock, peppercorns, sugar, and rice noodles and stir until combined.

At the last minute, add the crispy pork belly and stir-fry quickly until everything is fully combined. Check and adjust the seasoning, if necessary, and serve immediately, sprinkled with more Thai basil.

NOTES: *Lesser ginger is a rhizome related to galangal. If it is difficult to locate, substitute ginger.*

Thai basil is a variety of basil with a strong, spicy flavor. If you can't find it, you can substitute sweet basil.

The green peppercorns should be fresh, not dried. They can be found in most supermarkets, often with capers and other jarred items.

SPAGHETTI CARBONARA

Serves 4 to 6

1 pound fresh spaghetti

4 large eggs, beaten

Salt

½ cup heavy whipping cream

½ pound pancetta, chopped

1 tablespoon chopped garlic

Freshly ground black pepper

1 cup grated Parmigiano-Reggiano cheese (4 ounces)

1 tablespoon finely chopped fresh flat-leaf parsley

Fill a large pot with water, salt it, and bring it to a boil over high heat. Add the pasta and cook for 8 minutes, or until the pasta is al dente (cooked through but with a little resistance to the bite). Drain and set aside.

Season the beaten eggs with salt and add the cream.

In a large sauté pan over medium heat, cook the pancetta until crispy, about 6 minutes. Remove from the pan and drain on paper towels. Pour off all of the bacon fat except for 3 tablespoons. Add the

garlic, season with black pepper, and sauté for 30 seconds. Add the crispy pancetta and the cooked pasta and stir. Then add the egg mixture, stirring quickly until the eggs thicken into a sauce but do not scramble.

Remove the pan from the heat, add the cheese, and mix thoroughly. Garnish with the parsley and serve immediately.

BUCATINI WITH AMATRICIANA SAUCE

Serves 4 to 6

¼ cup extra-virgin olive oil

3 tablespoons unsalted butter

¼ pound bacon (preferably guanciale), cut into ¼-inch pieces (see Notes)

2 large red onions, finely diced

5 cloves garlic, sliced

1 tablespoon crushed red chili flakes

2 tablespoons tomato paste

1 cup trebbiano or other Italian unoaked dry white wine

1 (16-ounce) can San Marzano plum tomatoes, crushed by hand (see Notes)

Salt and freshly ground black pepper

1 pound bucatini pasta (preferably Rustichella d'Abruzzo brand)

12 ounces Pecorino Romano Locatelli, grated

Heat the olive oil and butter in a large skillet over medium-low heat. Cook the bacon until lightly browned and some of the fat has rendered out, about 5 minutes. Add the onions and garlic and cook until the bacon is fully rendered and the onions are slightly caramelized, about 12 minutes. Add the chili flakes and tomato paste and cook for about 10 minutes. Add the wine and cook for about 2 minutes. Add the crushed tomatoes and salt and pepper to taste, and simmer for 10 to 15 minutes. Check the seasoning and adjust if necessary.

Meanwhile, bring a large pot of salted water to a boil. Cook the pasta according to the package directions. Place the cooked pasta in the sauce and mix thoroughly. Add the grated cheese and serve.

NOTES: *Guanciale is the cheek or jowl cut of the pork, cured in the same way as traditional bacon (pork belly).*

San Marzano tomatoes are flavorful plum tomatoes from the San Marzano region of Italy; they are available in Italian specialty stores and some supermarkets.

"My good friend and sommelier at the restaurant, Richard Betts, wanted to hang out in the kitchen one night with me and make some late-night snacks. He asked for a pound of guanciale, good pasta, killer olive oil, and some of our heirloom purple garlic. Little did I know that on one of his extensive winemaking trips through the Italian countryside, he had been taught to make Amatriciana by an old Italian grandmother, and he shared his technique with me. It's a classic sauce that depends heavily on the ingredients you use. It's one of the comfort food dishes I make when it's snowing feet of snow outside!"

—CHEF RYAN HARDY

BACON MAC AND CHEESE

Serves 4 to 6

½ pound bacon

1 pound cavatelli pasta

1 bunch thyme (about the thickness of a quarter), plus 1½ tablespoons chopped, fresh thyme

4 sprigs rosemary

4 tablespoons (½ stick) unsalted butter

2 medium Spanish onions, coarsely chopped

1 clove garlic, crushed

½ to ¾ cup white wine

¼ to ½ cup all-purpose flour

4 cups milk

3 cups heavy whipping cream

¼ cup Dijon mustard

1 cup grated Grafton cheddar cheese (4 ounces; or other white cheddar)

¼ teaspoon freshly grated nutmeg

Salt and freshly ground black pepper

½ cup coarse breadcrumbs (cornbread is ideal)

1 cup grated Grana Padano cheese (4 ounces)

In a large skillet over medium-low heat, cook the bacon until crispy, about 10 minutes. Drain on paper towels. When cool, cut into ¼-inch pieces.

Preheat the oven to 350ºF. Bring a large pot of water to a boil. Add the pasta and cook until al dente. Drain and set aside.

Tie the bunch of thyme and sprigs of rosemary together with clean kitchen string. In a large wide-mouth stockpot, melt the butter over medium heat. Add the onions, garlic, and herbs and cook until the onion is soft, 8 to 10 minutes. Add the wine and cook, stirring occasionally, until reduced by half, about 10 minutes. Remove and discard the garlic and herbs. Whisk in the flour and cook, stirring, for 1 minute. Gradually whisk in the milk and cream, then the mustard. Reduce the heat to a gentle simmer and cook, stirring constantly, for about 30 minutes.

Remove the pan from the heat and stir in the cheddar, a handful at a time, waiting until each addition is completely melted before adding more. Season with the nutmeg and add salt and black pepper to taste.

Add the pasta, and the chopped thyme and bacon and heat through until the pasta is well coated and seasoned, about 5 minutes. Stir in the bacon pieces. Adjust the seasonings as needed.

Pour the mixture into a casserole dish or individual ovenproof gratin dishes. Sprinkle the top(s) with a generous layer of breadcrumbs, then a layer of Grana Padano, then another layer of breadcrumbs. Bake for 20 minutes, or until bubbly and crispy.

PASTA WITH BRUSSELS SPROUTS, CAULIFLOWER, HAZELNUTS, AND BACON

Serves 6

¼ pound thick-cut bacon, minced

1 sweet onion, diced

1 pint Brussels sprouts, trimmed and quartered

1 cup diced cauliflower

2 tablespoons olive oil

2 cloves garlic, minced

½ cup heavy whipping cream

¼ cup whole hazelnuts

1 pound medium or large tube pasta (such as penne or rigatoni)

¼ cup chopped fresh flat-leaf parsley

¼ cup grated Parmigiano-Reggiano cheese

Cook the bacon in a large skillet over medium-low heat for 10 minutes, until lightly browned. Remove the bacon from the pan and set it aside. To the rendered fat, add the onion, Brussels sprouts, cauliflower, and olive oil and cook until nicely browned, about 15 minutes.

Add the garlic, cream, and cooked bacon. Stir, and lower the heat to cook at a simmer for 15 minutes.

Preheat the oven to 400°F. In a small ovenproof skillet or on a baking sheet, toast the hazelnuts for 10 minutes. Cool, then remove the husks. (This is easier and less messy if you fold up the toasted hazelnuts in a clean kitchen towel and rub them vigorously. Most of the husks will stay behind in the towel.)

Fill a large pot with water, salt it, and bring it to a boil over high heat. Add the pasta and cook for 8 minutes, or until the pasta is al dente (cooked through but with a little resistance to the bite).

Add the pasta to the Brussels sprouts mixture in the pan and toss well. Add the toasted hazelnuts and the parsley. Toss again and adjust the seasoning, if necessary. Sprinkle with the cheese and serve hot.

FALL RISOTTO WITH ROASTED BUTTERNUT SQUASH AND DOUBLE-SMOKED BACON

Serves 6

1 butternut squash, peeled, seeded, and diced

¼ cup extra-virgin olive oil

Salt and freshly ground black pepper

½ pound applewood double-smoked bacon, diced

12 fresh sage leaves, plus ½ small bunch sage, stemmed, leaves julienned

1 large red onion, diced

1½ cups Arborio rice

1 cup white wine

6 cups chicken stock, hot

½ cup pecan halves, toasted, then crushed

¼ cup chopped fresh flat-leaf parsley

1 cup (2 sticks) unsalted butter, cut into ½-inch pieces

½ cup shaved Parmigiano-Reggiano cheese, for garnish

Preheat the oven to 350°F.

Fill a large saucepan halfway with water and bring to a boil over medium-high heat. Add the squash and cook until tender, about 15 minutes. Use a slotted spoon to transfer the squash to a baking sheet, then coat with the 2 tablespoons olive oil and season with salt and black pepper. Roast for about 10 minutes, or until lightly browned.

In a medium skillet over medium-low heat, cook the bacon pieces until crispy, about 10 minutes. Drain on paper towels and set aside. Fry the 12 sage leaves in the bacon fat until crispy, about 3 minutes, then drain on paper towels and season with salt. Set aside.

Heat the remaining 2 tablespoons of olive oil in a large pot over medium heat. Add the onion and cook until tender, about 5 minutes. Add the rice and stir to coat with oil. Add the white wine and cook, stirring, until the wine is absorbed. Add the hot chicken stock 1 ladle at a time, stirring constantly, until each ladleful is absorbed. This should take about 20 minutes total. About 15 minutes into it, and before adding the last ladle of hot stock, add the squash, bacon, pecans, julienned sage, and parsley. After the last ladle of stock is absorbed, add the butter and stir until melted and creamy. Check the seasoning and add salt and pepper to taste. Garnish with the fried sage leaves and shaved cheese and serve.

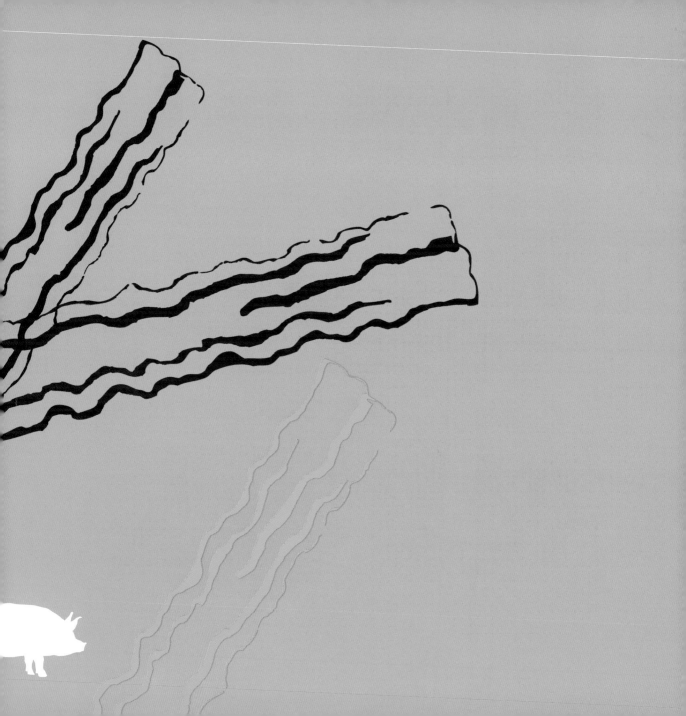

FISH

Scallops with Dried Cranberries and Bacon 65

Halibut with Soy-Ginger Braised Bacon
and Bok Choy with Red Miso Sauce 67

Bluefish with Corn, Avocado, and Bacon Salad 69

Pancetta-Wrapped Monkfish
with Cauliflower Flan, Asparagus, and Morels 70

Whole Roasted Branzino
with Carrots and Bacon 73

CHEF ANDY HUSBANDS AND JOE YONAN, **TREMONT 647, BOSTON, MASSACHUSETTS**

SCALLOPS WITH DRIED CRANBERRIES AND BACON

Serves 4

	AÏOLI	SCALLOPS
1 tablespoon olive oil	1 large egg	1½ pounds large sea scallops
6 slices bacon, minced	1 tablespoon freshly squeezed lemon juice	2 tablespoons canola oil, or a mixture 1 tablespoon canola oil and 1 tablespoon rendered bacon fat
1 cup dried cranberries	2 cloves garlic, coarsely chopped	¼ cup coarsely chopped flat-leaf parsley
½ cup warm water	2 teaspoons Dijon mustard	
¼ cup Tabasco sauce	1 cup canola oil	
	Salt and freshly ground black pepper	
	1 tablespoon maple syrup (preferably Vermont)	

Heat the olive oil in a large sauté pan (preferably nonstick) over medium heat and cook the bacon, stirring frequently, until browned and crunchy, 6 to 8 minutes. Reserve 1 tablespoon of the rendered bacon fat for the aïoli. If desired, reserve the rest of the rendered fat for searing the scallops.

In a small bowl, combine the cranberries, water, and Tabasco and soak for at least 20 minutes.

To make the aïoli, put the egg, lemon juice, garlic, and mustard in a food processor or blender and puree until smooth. Combine all but 1 tablespoon of the canola oil with the 1 tablespoon of rendered bacon fat. Slowly drizzle the canola oil (or canola and bacon fat) into the food processor while it is running until the aïoli is smooth, thick, and shiny. Transfer the aïoli to a small bowl and season with salt and pepper to taste. Add the maple syrup and mix thoroughly. Set aside.

Season the scallops with salt and black pepper. Heat the canola oil in a large sauté pan over high heat. Carefully place the scallops in the pan, then reduce the heat to medium-high. Sear the scallops until they have developed a golden brown crust on each side, 2 to 3 minutes per side.

Strain the cranberries and discard the liquid. Place some scallops in the center of each plate. Sprinkle the cranberries and bacon pieces on top. Use a spoon to drizzle the maple aioli in a crisscross pattern over all. Garnish with the parsley and serve immediately.

NOTE: *This can also serve 4 to 6 people as an appetizer. The aïoli recipe makes 2 cups, but you only need about ¼ cup here. The leftover aïoli will keep, covered, in the refrigerator for up to 1 week and can also be used in sandwiches.*

HALIBUT WITH SOY-GINGER BRAISED BACON AND BOK CHOY WITH RED MISO SAUCE

Serves 4

SOY CARAMEL

½ cup sugar

½ cup soy sauce

HALIBUT CHEEKS

¼ cup extra-virgin olive oil

8 (3-ounce) halibut cheeks

Salt and freshly ground black pepper

8 tablespoons (1 stick) butter, cut into ½-inch pieces

12 sprigs thyme

1 pound Soy-Ginger Bacon, cut into 4 equal pieces (page 5)

RED MISO SAUCE

2 tablespoons olive oil

1 medium onion, diced

1 large carrot, chopped

2 red bell peppers, cored, seeded, and diced

2 tablespoons chopped fresh ginger

3 cloves garlic, smashed

1 cup red shiro miso

1 tablespoon sugar

4 cups vegetable stock

1 teaspoon soy lecithin (see Notes)

To make the soy caramel, combine the sugar and soy sauce in a small saucepan and bring to a simmer over medium heat. Continue to cook until the mixture thickens into a dark syrup, about 10 minutes. Remove from the heat and set aside to cool for 10 minutes before transferring it to a nonreactive container with a tight-fitting lid. Set aside.

To prepare the halibut, heat the olive oil in a large skillet over medium-high heat. Pat the cheeks dry with a paper towel and season them with salt and black pepper. Place them in the hot oil. Do not crowd the pan, as they will steam and not develop a good crust. Cook, without touching or turning, for 3 minutes, or until a nice crust has formed on the bottom side. Using tongs, turn the fish pieces over and brown the other side. Turn off the heat and add the butter and thyme. Tipping the pan slightly so the butter collects on one end, spoon the hot butter over the fish, basting them for 1 minute. Transfer the fish to paper towels to drain and rest while you repeat the process with subsequent batches.

Use the same pan to cook the bacon. Pat the bacon with a paper towel and cook for 1 to 2 minutes on each side, until browned. Remove from the pan and set aside on paper towels.

To make the red miso sauce, heat the 2 tablespoons olive oil in a medium saucepan over medium-high heat. When the oil is hot, add the onion, carrot, and bell peppers and cook until they start to develop some color, 5 to 7 minutes. Stir in the garlic and cook until it starts to soften, about 1 minute. Stir in the miso and sugar to coat the vegetables. Reduce the heat to medium and continue to cook until the sugar has dissolved and the vegetables begin to caramelize, about 1 minute. Add the stock and lower the heat to medium-low. Bring the mixture to a simmer and cook for 45 minutes, or until the liquid is reduced by half.

Strain the contents through a fine-mesh sieve into a bowl. Discard the solids.

When you are ready to serve, add the soy lecithin to the hot liquid and whip the mixture with a hand-held mixer until a heavy froth forms.

Drizzle the soy caramel across the middle of each of 4 serving plates. Divide the halibut cheeks and sliced bacon evenly among the plates, placing them on top of and around the soy caramel. Top each plate with a couple of spoonfuls of frothy red miso sauce and serve.

NOTES: *This dish brings together a yin and yang of sweet and salty elements: the natural sweetness of the sea in the halibut cheeks with the savory smokiness of the land in the bacon; the sugar and soy sauce; and the alluringly sweet yet meaty flavor of red miso. The back-and-forth tug of flavors is addictive. This recipe also works well with scallops.*

Lecithin is sold as a food supplement and for medical uses. In cooking, it is often used as an emulsifier, especially for chocolate and candy.

BLUEFISH WITH CORN, AVOCADO, AND BACON SALAD

Serves 6

1 pound smoked bacon, cut into small cubes

2 pounds bluefish fillets, cut into 6 equal portions

Salt and freshly ground black pepper

2 ears corn, cooked, kernels cut off the cobs

1 ripe Hass avocado, pitted, peeled, and cubed

1 small red onion, sliced

1 pound cherry tomatoes, halved

1 jalapeño chile, seeded and sliced

1 bunch cilantro, stemmed

Juice of 1 lime

Preheat the oven to 400°F.

Cook the bacon in a large ovenproof skillet over low heat until the fat is rendered, turn over after 5 minutes and cook on the other side for about 5 more minutes, until crispy. Transfer the bacon and half of the rendered fat to a large bowl. Leave the remaining bacon fat in the skillet.

Season the fish with salt and pepper and put it skin side down in the hot pan with the remaining bacon fat. Transfer to the oven and bake to your desired doneness. Medium-rare will take close to 5 minutes; well-done closer to 10 minutes.

Add the corn, avocado, red onion, cherry tomatoes, jalapeño, cilantro, and lime juice to the cooked bacon in the bowl and toss to make a warm salad. Spoon the salad onto 6 plates, top with pieces of the bluefish, and serve.

PANCETTA-WRAPPED MONKFISH WITH CAULIFLOWER FLAN, ASPARAGUS, AND MORELS

Serves 6

30 ounces monkfish, trimmed and cut into 6 (5-ounce) portions

24 thin slices pancetta or bacon (see Notes)

24 jumbo asparagus spears, peeled and trimmed

¾ cup (1½ sticks) butter

1 large shallot, minced

2 cloves garlic, minced

30 medium to small morel mushrooms, carefully washed and dried (see Notes)

¼ cup Madeira (see Note)

2 tablespoons vegetable oil

2 cups chicken stock

1 teaspoon chopped fresh chervil

1 teaspoon chopped fresh flat-leaf parsley

Kosher salt and freshly cracked black pepper

Cauliflower Flans, for serving (recipe follows)

Wrap each portion of monkfish with 4 strips of pancetta to completely cover the fish. Wrap each with parchment paper and refrigerate for 3 to 4 hours. Go ahead and prepare the Cauliflower Flans.

Bring a pot of salted water to a boil, and blanch the asparagus until just cooked, 3 to 5 minutes. Transfer to a bowl of ice water to stop the cooking. Drain and set aside.

Melt 2 tablespoons of the butter in a medium sauté pan over medium-high heat. When bubbling, add the shallot and garlic and cook for 1 minute. Add the morels and sauté for 3 to 5 minutes, until the mixture begins to brown. Add the Madeira and deglaze the pan by stirring up the bits stuck to the bottom, then cook until almost all of the liquid is

evaporated, which will take only a few minutes. Keep warm.

Preheat the oven to 375°F.

In an ovenproof sauté pan large enough to hold all the monkfish, heat the vegetable oil over medium-high heat. When hot, add the pancetta-wrapped monkfish and brown on all sides, 5 to 7 minutes. Transfer to the oven and bake for 3 to 5 minutes. Remove the fish from the pan and set aside. Without wiping out the pan, add the chicken stock and cook over high heat until reduced by half, about 15 minutes. Add 4 tablespoons of the butter and the morel mixture and bring to a boil. Add the chervil and parsley and keep warm.

Melt the remaining 6 tablespoons of butter in a large sauté pan and cook the asparagus over medium heat for 5 minutes. Season with salt and pepper to taste.

To serve, cut each piece of monkfish in half, and place 2 halves on each of 6 warm serving plates. Invert 1 warm cauliflower flan on each plate and add 4 spears of asparagus, fanned out, and top with the morel and chervil-parsley butter.

NOTES: *Pancetta is an Italian dry cured meat, similar to bacon. It is pork belly that has been salt cured and spiced and dried for about 3 months (but usually not smoked).*

Madeira is a fortified Portuguese wine often used in cooking.

CAULIFLOWER FLANS

Makes 6 flans

4 tablespoons (½ stick) butter

½ small head cauliflower, cut into florets (about 2 cups)

½ cup heavy whipping cream, or more as needed

½ cup milk

2 cloves garlic, peeled

¼ teaspoon kosher salt

½ teaspoon freshly ground white pepper

3 large whole eggs, plus 2 large yolks

¼ cup grated Parmigiano-Reggiano cheese

Heat 4 tablespoons of the butter in a sauté pan over medium heat and cook the cauliflower florets, turning frequently, until all are browned and just tender, 5 to 8 minutes.

In a large saucepan over high heat, bring the cauliflower, cream, milk, garlic, salt, and white pepper to a boil. Add a little more cream if necessary to completely cover the cauliflower. Cook until the cauliflower is very tender, about 8 minutes. Strain the cauliflower and return the liquid to the pan. Cook, stirring, over medium heat, until reduced to 1 cup. Remove from the heat and let cool.

Puree the liquid and cooked cauliflower in a blender until very smooth. Add the whole eggs, yolks, and cheese and blend. It should make about 2 cups. The flan mixture can be prepared to this point a day ahead. Store in the refrigerator in a covered bowl.

Preheat the oven to 275ºF. Spray 6 flan molds with nonstick cooking spray.

Fill the molds four-fifths of the way to the top. Place the molds in a large roasting pan, and then add water to reach half way up the sides of the molds. Bake for 1 hour, or until a toothpick inserted into the flans comes out clean.

WHOLE ROASTED BRANZINO WITH CARROTS AND BACON

Serves 4

2 whole small branzini (see Note)

Salt and freshly ground black pepper

1 cup olive oil

12 cloves garlic, peeled

8 carrots, diced

2 cups (4 sticks) unsalted butter

1 pound bacon, diced

1 cup white wine

2 cups chicken stock

Juice of 4 lemons

Preheat the oven to 375°F.

Season the fish with salt and pepper. Heat the olive oil in a large ovenproof sauté pan over medium-high heat until it just starts to smoke. Add the fish and sear on one side until golden brown, 8 to 10 minutes. Flip the fish and add the garlic cloves, carrots, 2 sticks of the butter, and the bacon. Bake for 10 minutes.

Remove the pan from the oven and, leaving the fish and vegetables in the pan, drain off the excess fat. Place the pan back on the stovetop over medium heat. Add the white wine, cook for 3 minutes, then add the chicken stock, lemon juice, and the remaining 2 sticks of butter. Stir and cook for 3 minutes more, so that everything melds into a sauce. Season with salt and pepper to taste, and serve.

NOTE: *Chef Allen often prepares this dish with baby monkfish, which can be difficult to find. Branzino, a delicious alternative, is Mediterranean sea bass. Depending on the size of the fish, you may need to use two large fish and cook them in two separate pans.*

MEAT

Bacon-Wrapped Pork Tenderloin
with Clams and Sweet Peas 77

Veal and Foie Gras Meatloaf Wrapped in Bacon 78

Caramel Braised Pork with Pineapple 79

New England Baked Beans with Bacon Crust 81

Tartiflette 83

Higado de Res Especial
(Special Smothered Liver with Bacon and Onions) 84

Smoked Bacon Tempura with Grilled Corn Salad 86

Tacos Al Pastor (Bacon Tacos) 87

Bacon and Sauerkraut Stew
with Cucumber Salad 90

BACON-WRAPPED PORK TENDERLOIN WITH CLAMS AND SWEET PEAS

Serves 2

10 ounces pork tenderloin

Salt and freshly ground black pepper

½ pound sliced bacon

2 tablespoons canola oil

1 shallot, minced

1 small clove garlic, minced

12 Manila clams, or small littlenecks (see Note)

2 tablespoons white wine

14 sugar snap peas, strings removed

1 tablespoon unsalted butter

¼ cup shelled peas

1 cup pea leaves or pea sprouts (optional)

3 fresh mint leaves, julienned

2 fresh basil leaves, julienned

Freshly squeezed lemon juice, for serving

Lightly season the pork with salt and pepper. Lay the bacon out on a work surface so that it is just overlapping and creates a square the length of the pork. Place the pork on top and wrap the pork so that the ends of the bacon overlap to create a seal.

Heat a large sauté pan over high heat. When hot, add the canola oil, then the wrapped pork. Reduce the heat to medium-high and cook, turning, until browned on all sides, 8 to 10 minutes. Transfer the meat to a warm plate.

Add the shallot and garlic to the pan and stir. Add the clams and white wine, cover, and cook just until the clams open, about 5 minutes. Remove the clams and set them aside, discarding any that do not open. Return any accumulated juices from the plate with the pork to the pan and increase the heat to high. Reduce slightly, then add the sugar snap peas and butter and toss. Add the English peas and pea leaves and stir until wilted and the peas are bright green, about 5 minutes.

Cut the pork into 1-inch-thick slices. Divide the pea mixture between 2 warm plates, sprinkle the mint and basil on top, top with the sliced pork and clams, and serve.

NOTE: *Manila clams are small oval clams from the Pacific Ocean, widely used in Japan.*

CHEF MARK ALLEN, **LE SOIR, BOSTON, MASSACHUSETTS**

VEAL AND FOIE GRAS MEATLOAF WRAPPED IN BACON

Serves 6

1 cup olive oil

1 large white onion, diced

¼ cup minced garlic

½ pound foie gras

3 pounds freshly ground veal

½ cup chopped fresh flat-leaf parsley

¼ cup chopped fresh thyme

½ cup fresh breadcrumbs

3 large eggs

½ cup molasses

½ cup ketchup or tomato sauce

2 tablespoons Worcestershire sauce

1 tablespoon Tabasco sauce

15 slices thick-cut bacon

Salt and freshly ground black pepper

Heat ¼ cup of the olive oil in a large sauté pan over medium heat and sauté the onion and garlic until tender, about 10 minutes. Set aside and let cool.

Preheat the oven to 350°F.

Puree the foie gras in a food processor.

In a large bowl, combine the veal, foie gras, parsley, thyme, breadcrumbs, eggs, molasses, ketchup, Worcestershire, Tabasco, the remaining ¾ cup olive oil, and the cooled onion mixture and mix well. Transfer the mixture to a work surface, form it into a free-form oblong shape, and set it aside.

Lay each piece of the bacon flat on a baking sheet, overlapping the edges one on top of another to cover the length of the free-form meatloaf. Place the meatloaf in the center of the bacon and wrap the ends of the bacon up and around the meatloaf, so it is completely encased. Bake for 1 hour. Let rest for 10 minutes before slicing and serving.

CARAMEL BRAISED PORK WITH PINEAPPLE

Serves 4

½ cup plus 2 tablespoons sugar

1 tablespoon freshly squeezed lemon juice

2 tablespoons water

3 tablespoons soy sauce

3 tablespoons nam pla (fish sauce)

1 medium sweet potato, peeled and cut into ½-inch cubes

1 cup pineapple, cut into ½-inch cubes, with juices

½ cup sake or white wine

1 tablespoon coarsely ground black pepper, plus more for serving

8 peeled, round, thin slices fresh ginger

2 green onion ends, with roots, plus 1 green onion, sliced and thinly julienned, for garnish

Salt

2 pounds pork belly, cut into ½-inch-thick slices

Preheat the oven to 350°F.

In a large ovenproof widemouthed pot, mix together the sugar, lemon juice, and water until it resembles wet sand. Use a clean pastry brush dipped in water to clean the sides of the pot and remove any residual sugar. Cook over high heat, stirring occasionally, until the mixture turns to dark caramel, about 15 minutes.

Meanwhile, mix together in a medium bowl the soy sauce, fish sauce, sweet potato, pineapple with juice, wine, black pepper, ginger, and green onion ends. When the caramel is dark, slowly and carefully add the soy sauce mixture to the pot to stop the cooking process. Bring the mixture to a boil again. Taste the sauce, and add more sugar, if necessary, as the sweetness of the pineapple can vary. Add salt to taste.

Turn off the heat, and place the pieces of pork in the caramel. The caramel should come at least two-thirds of the way up the pork pieces; change to a smaller pot if necessary. Fold the mixture so that the pineapple is on top of the pork. Place in the preheated oven and cook for 15 to18 minutes, or until the pork is tender. Transfer the pork pieces to a plate.

Bring the remaining mixture in the pot to a boil again on the stovetop and cook until thickened, about 15 minutes. Spoon the sauce with pineapple chunks on top of the pork and garnish with the julienned green onion. Sprinkle with freshly cracked black pepper and serve immediately.

EXECUTIVE CHEF BRADFORD THOMPSON, BELLYFULL CONSULTING, NEW YORK, NEW YORK

NEW ENGLAND BAKED BEANS WITH BACON CRUST

Serves 6

1 pound dried navy beans or white beans (see Note)

1 medium sweet white onion, quartered, plus 2 cups diced sweet white onion

1 large carrot, halved, plus 1 cup diced carrot

1 head garlic, split, plus 3 cloves garlic, grated on a Microplane grater

1 bay leaf

½ sprig rosemary

2 sprigs thyme, chopped, plus 2 whole sprigs

1 tablespoon salt, plus more for seasoning

5 medium tomatoes, seeded and quartered

3 tablespoons olive oil

¼ cup water

2 cups cubed smoked bacon (1 by ½ by ½-inch batons)

1 cup diced turnip

½ cup diced celery

Freshly ground black pepper

¼ cup molasses

1 (12-ounce) bottle dark beer

12 (¼-inch) slices flat pancetta

¼ cup loosely packed light brown sugar

Crusty bread, for serving

Place the beans in a large stockpot, cover them with water, and soak overnight. The next day, drain off the water, rinse and drain the beans, add them back to the stockpot, and add the quartered onion, halved carrot, and split head of garlic. Cover the mixture with cold water, add the bay leaf, rosemary, and 2 sprigs of thyme, place the pot over medium heat, and cook for 1 to 1½ hours, until the beans are tender. Remove and discard the vegetables and herbs, stir in 1 tablespoon of salt, then transfer the beans, with their liquid, to a large dish to cool.

Meanwhile, preheat the oven to 300°F.

In a mixing bowl, toss the tomatoes with the olive oil, chopped thyme, and some salt. Transfer the mixture to a baking sheet and bake for 1 to 1½ hours, until the tomatoes are slightly dried out. Set aside, and increase the oven temperature to 325°F.

Place the ¼ cup of water and the smoked bacon in a large saucepan and cook over medium heat to render the bacon, 7 to 9 minutes. When the bacon is rendered, transfer it to a tray and remove all but 2 tablespoons of the fat from the pan. Add the diced onion to the fat and cook over medium-high heat until the onion begins to color, about 5 minutes. Add the turnip and diced carrot to the saucepan and cook for 5 minutes longer. Add the celery and grated garlic and cook for 3 minutes longer. Give it a good stir, season with a little salt and black pepper, add the molasses, and cook for 2 to 3 minutes. Stir in the beer. Cook until the liquid is reduced by half, about 5 minutes. Stir in the bacon beans, with liquid, and tomatoes. Reduce the heat to medium-low and simmer for 5 to 6 minutes.

Line a casserole dish, or ideally a bean pot, with the pancetta slices. Do this by placing the narrower end of the slice into the pot and draping the thick end outside of the pot. Carefully pour the beans into the pot, then fold the ends of the pancetta slices over the top, overlapping each piece. Sprinkle the brown sugar evenly over the top and place the pot, uncovered, in the oven. Bake for about 1½ hours, or until the top is crispy and browned. Serve hot with crusty bread.

NOTE: *The beans must be soaked overnight, so you'll need to plan accordingly.*

TARTIFLETTE

Serves 8

10 Yukon gold potatoes, peeled and diced into ½-inch pieces

1 pound bacon, cut into 1 by ½-inch pieces

2 large yellow onions, minced

2 cups heavy whipped cream

4 cups grated Mountain Tomme cheese (1 pound; see Notes)

2 tablespoons fresh thyme leaves

Salt and freshly ground black pepper

1½ pounds finocchiona (see Notes)

2 baguettes (preferably from La Brea Bakery)

Fill a large pot with water, salt it, add the potatoes, and bring to a boil over medium heat. Boil until the potatoes are tender, about 15 minutes. Drain the potatoes.

In a large skillet over medium heat, cook the bacon until crispy, about 10 minutes. Drain off any excess fat, then add the onions and cook until caramelized, 10 to 12 minutes. Add the potatoes and brown them slightly, 10 to 12 minutes. Stir in the cream. Turn off the heat and add the cheese and thyme. Season to taste with salt and black pepper.

Serve hot with thinly sliced finocchiona and baguettes.

NOTES: *Tartiflette is a classic dish from the Savoie valley of France. Chef Hardy uses The Little Nell's homemade bacon and homemade alpine Tomme cow's milk cheese (it pays to own a farm!). It was developed by his chef de cuisine (at the time) Andrew Helsley, who adapted it from a friend of his, so in a sense it's a family heirloom. You can substitute just about any creamy and/or slightly stinky cheese. Semisoft cow's cheeses such as Tomme de Savoie, Reblochon, and Taleggio work very well.*

Finocchiona is a mild Tuscan pork salami that contains fennel seed instead of peppercorn. For this recipe, Chef Hardy uses The Little Nell house prepared salami.

CHEF/OWNER ZARELA MARTINEZ, ZARELA RESTAURANT, NEW YORK, NEW YORK

HIGADO DE RES ESPECIAL (SPECIAL SMOTHERED LIVER WITH BACON AND ONIONS)

Serves 4 to 8

½ pound bacon

8 (½-inch-thick) slices calves' liver

4 cups boiling water

1 tablespoon vinegar

2 tablespoons Worcestershire sauce

4 cloves garlic, minced

Salt and freshly ground black pepper

3 tablespoons olive oil

1 large onion, cut into thin half-moons

All-purpose flour, for dredging

Pickled serrano or jalapeño chiles, for serving

Place the bacon in a large skillet over medium-low heat and cook for 5 minutes. Turn the bacon and cook on the other side for 2 to 5 minutes, or until crispy. Drain on paper towels. Set aside. Save the rendered fat and wipe out the pan.

Place the slices of liver in a large bowl and pour the boiling water over them. When grayish in color, remove the liver from the hot water and remove the skin from the edges of the slices.

In a wide, shallow bowl, whisk together the vinegar, Worcestershire, garlic, and salt and black pepper. Place the liver in the mixture, toss to coat it, and let marinate in the refrigerator for at least 30 minutes.

Heat the olive oil in the skillet over medium-high heat until rippling. Add the onion and stir well to coat with the oil. Adjust the heat to low, cover the pan, and cook the onion, stirring occasionally, until wilted and lightly browned, about 10 minutes. Transfer to a plate and set aside.

Place the flour for dredging on a large plate. Remove the liver from the marinade and dredge it in the flour. Brown it in the skillet in the reserved bacon fat over medium heat for about 1 minute on each side. Reduce the heat to low and cook for 10 minutes, turning only once halfway through and being careful not to overcook it. Serve covered with the crispy whole bacon slices and sautéed onion, with pickled chiles on the side.

"There were many great cooks on both sides of my family. This recipe was taught to me by one of my father's aunts. She was married to an American gentleman, and when I use that term I mean a gentle man. My Uncle Bob, who came from Texas pioneer stock, was well known and respected all over the parts of Arizona and Mexico where I grew up. My dad used to say that he was tops as an appraiser of beef on the hoof. He married my Aunt Josephine long before I was born. My aunt's mother-in-law used to fix liver this way, and I have converted many a liver hater with precisely this recipe."

—CHEF MARTINEZ

SMOKED BACON TEMPURA WITH GRILLED CORN SALAD

Serves 4

GRILLED CORN SALAD

2 cups grilled corn (from 3 to 4 cobs, depending on size)

¼ cup julienned sugar snap peas

¼ cup julienned red onion

¼ cup diced red bell pepper

2 tablespoons chopped fresh cilantro

Juice of 2 lemons

¼ cup extra-virgin olive oil

CHIPOTLE MAYONNAISE

2 egg yolks

Juice of 4 limes

1 cup canola oil

1 chipotle dried chile, seeded and chopped

3 cups all-purpose flour

2⅓ cups plus ½ cup club soda

4 egg whites

2 quarts canola oil, for frying

12 slices thick-cut applewood-smoked bacon (see Note)

Salt and freshly ground black pepper

To prepare the corn salad, combine the grilled corn, sugar snap peas, onion, red bell pepper, cilantro, lemon juice, and olive oil in a large bowl and mix well. The salad may be refrigerated for up to 2 days before using.

To prepare the chipotle mayonnaise, combine the egg yolks, lime juice, and canola oil in a blender and puree until the mixture emulsifies. Add the chipotle and puree until blended. Keep cold until ready to serve.

In a wide bowl, mix the flour and club soda. In a large bowl, whisk the egg whites with an electric mixer until they form soft peaks, 3 to 5 minutes. Fold the egg whites into the flour mixture. Heat the canola oil in a large pot to 350°F on a deep-frying thermometer.

Coat the slices of bacon on each side with the batter, then carefully drop them in the hot oil, making sure not to crowd them, as the pot may overflow and the bacon will not cook evenly. As each piece of bacon tempura becomes golden brown, remove it with a slotted spoon, drain on paper towels, and immediately season it with salt and pepper.

Serve the tempura warm, with the chipotle mayonnaise on the side for dipping and accompanied by the corn salad.

NOTE: *Chef McDaniel prefers bacon from North Country Smokehouse in Claremont, New Hampshire.*

TACOS AL PASTOR (BACON TACOS)

Serves 4 to 6

TOMATILLO SALSA

5 medium to large tomatillos, husked and quartered (see Notes)

1 small white onion, quartered

2 jalapeño chiles, stemmed, seeded, and quartered

1 large bunch cilantro

2 cloves garlic, peeled

¼ cup water

Kosher salt

ADOBO SAUCE

2 tablespoons olive oil

1 Spanish onion, roughly sliced and chopped

3 cloves garlic, peeled

1 cinnamon stick

1 bay leaf

½ teaspoon dried oregano

½ teaspoon ground cumin

1 canned chipotle chile in adobo sauce (see Notes)

10 dried guajillo chiles, stemmed, seeded, and deveined

5 cups water

1 cup pineapple juice

¼ cup sherry vinegar

PORK AL PASTOR

3 pounds Berkshire pork belly

½ cup diced fresh pineapple

TO SERVE

10 corn tortillas

½ cup diced Spanish onion

1 avocado, pitted, peeled, and cut lengthwise into 12 wedges

¼ cup chopped fresh cilantro

2 limes, quartered

To prepare the tomatillo salsa, place the tomatillos, onion, jalapeños, cilantro, garlic cloves, and water in a blender or food processor. Pulse until the purée is mostly smooth, about 2 minutes. Season to taste with salt and set aside.

To prepare the adobo sauce, heat the olive oil in a small pan over medium heat. Sauté the onion and garlic until translucent, then add the cinnamon stick, bay leaf, oregano, cumin, and chipotle and cook for about 2 minutes. Then add the guajillo chiles, water, and pineapple juice and season with salt. Cook over medium heat until the guajillos are tender, about 10 minutes. Set the pan aside to cool. When the liquid is cool enough, pulse the mixture in a blender until it forms a smooth paste. Add the sherry vinegar and more salt if needed. Set aside.

Preheat the oven to 375°F. Cut the pork belly into 6 steaks and rub each one with some of the adobo sauce and some salt. Place the steaks in a large baking dish and distribute the diced pineapple in between the steaks. Pour the rest of the adobo sauce over the top and bake for about 1 hour, until

the pork is tender and fully cooked. Remove the pan from the oven and cut the pork al pastor into ½-inch slices.

Heat the corn tortillas on a griddle. (You may want to do this step ahead and keep them warm on a plate in the oven.) Fill each tortilla with 3 or 4 slices of pork al pastor, and top with the diced onion, avocado, cilantro, and tomatillo salsa. Serve with the lime quarters for squeezing over the tacos.

NOTES: *Tomatillos, which are sometimes referred to as green tomatoes (the Spanish* tomate verde*) in Mexico, are related to the cape gooseberry, bearing small, spherical, green or green-purple fruit of the same name. Tomatillos are grown throughout the Western Hemisphere. Many grocery stores carry them.*

Adobo is a sauce with tomatoes, garlic, vinegar, salt, and spices. It is traditionally used in Latin cooking.

CHEF WAYNE NISH, **RESTAURATEUR AT MARCHONE, LTD, SINGAPORE**

BACON AND SAUERKRAUT STEW WITH CUCUMBER SALAD

Serves 6 to 8

2½ pounds sauerkraut (preferably imported German or Polish sauerkraut)

1¼ pounds fresh meaty belly bacon, cut into 2 pieces lengthwise

2 tablespoons vegetable oil

½ pound sliced Irish back bacon, cut into ½-inch pieces (see Notes)

2 tablespoons caraway seeds

6 bay leaves

½ teaspoon freshly ground black pepper

1 teaspoon sea salt

2½ pounds yellow onions, halved, ends cut off, and thinly sliced

2 ripe plum tomatoes, cored but not peeled or seeded, diced

1¼ pounds smoked slab bacon, cut in 2 pieces lengthwise

1¼ pounds small new potatoes (1 inch in diameter or cut to that size)

1 pint (500 milliliters) weissbier (white beer), lager, or pilsner

Cucumber Salad (recipe follows)

Soak the sauerkraut in cold water to cover for at least 1 hour, or up to overnight. Drain well.

Bring a medium pot of water to a boil. Blanch the belly bacon in the boiling water for 10 minutes. Drain and set aside.

Heat the vegetable oil in a heavy 8-quart pot over low heat and sauté the Irish back bacon with the caraway seeds, bay leaves, and black pepper for 5 minutes, stirring well to prevent sticking. Add the salt, onions, and tomatoes and cook for 10 to 15 minutes more, or until the onion is soft and transparent. Add the sauerkraut to the pot and mix well.

Remove half of the mixture from the pot and place the blanched bacon, smoked slab bacon, and potatoes on top of the mixture in the pot. Return the rest of the mixture to the pot and pour in the beer. Bring to a simmer, cover, and cook gently for 3 hours. Let rest for 1 hour off the heat to allow the flavors to meld.

Remove the meats and carve them into ½-inch slices. Spoon the sauerkraut and potato mixture onto a large platter and arrange the sliced meats on top. Serve hot with the cucumber salad.

NOTES: *Irish back bacon is made from the back of the pig rather than the belly.*

This stew is great served with mustard (preferably imported German or Polish mustard with horseradish), rye bread, sweet butter, and Cucumber Salad (recipe follows). Beer pairing suggestions: weissbier, lager or pilsner beer, German riesling, or Alsatian pinot gris.

CUCUMBER SALAD

1 pound cucumbers, thinly sliced

½ teaspoon sea salt or kosher salt

2 tablespoons champagne or apple cider vinegar

½ cup sour cream

1 tablespoon fresh dill, minced

Place the sliced cucumbers in a colander set over a bowl and sprinkle them with the salt. Let drain for 30 minutes. Mix the cucumbers in a medium bowl with the vinegar, sour cream, and dill and serve.

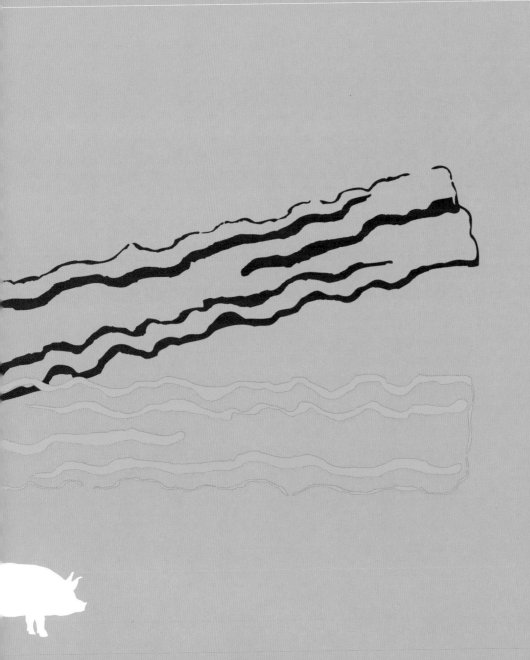

DESSERTS

Caramelized Bacon Brioche with
Apple-Bacon Confit and Bacon Candy 94
Chocolate-Dipped Smoked Almond-Bacon Brittle 97
BaCorn (Bacon-Caramel Popcorn
with Chile-Spiked Peanuts) 98
Chocolate-Bacon Cupcakes 99
Cane Sugar and Bacon-Iced Cupcakes 102
Bacon Panna Cotta with Huckleberries 104
Maple-Bacon Ice Cream 105
Pig Candy Ice Cream 106

CARAMELIZED BACON BRIOCHE WITH APPLE-BACON CONFIT AND BACON CANDY

Serves 4

BACON CANDY

10 slices bacon

½ cup loosely packed brown sugar

CARAMELIZED BACON BRIOCHE

1 loaf brioche bread

4 cups half-and-half

2 cups loosely packed brown sugar

1 tablespoon ground cinnamon

1 teaspoon ground nutmeg

½ teaspoon ground ginger

Pinch of salt

10 large eggs, slightly beaten

APPLE-BACON CONFIT

3 slices bacon, diced

1½ cups loosely packed brown sugar

Juice of 2 lemons

1 cinnamon stick

1 vanilla bean, split and scraped

7 Gala apples, peeled, cored, and diced

1 pint vanilla ice cream, for serving

One day ahead, make the bacon candy. Preheat the oven to 375°F and line a baking sheet with parchment paper. Lay the bacon on the baking sheet. Cover each piece of bacon with a thin layer of the brown sugar and bake for 10 minutes, or until crispy. Crumble 6 pieces of the caramelized bacon for the brioche mixture, and leave the remaining 4 slices whole.

Also one day ahead, begin making the brioche mixture. Using a serrated knife, slice the brioche into ¼-inch-thick slices. Cut each slice in half and trim the crust off so you have rectangular pieces. Leave uncovered overnight to dry out. Combine the half-and-half, brown sugar, cinnamon, nutmeg, ginger, and salt in a medium saucepan and cook over medium heat until simmering, about 10 minutes. Temper in the eggs by adding them slowly and stirring constantly, and remove from the heat. Add the crumbled bacon candy bits. Cover and refrigerate the mixture overnight.

To make the apple-bacon confit, sauté the bacon in a medium saucepan over medium heat until the fat begins to render, about 5 minutes. Drain off the fat and reserve it for frying the brioche. Add the brown sugar, lemon juice, cinnamon stick, and vanilla to the pan and stir to combine. Add the apples and cook over low heat until they become soft and translucent, about 10 minutes. Remove the pan from the heat and set it aside.

Skim the fat off the top of the chilled egg mixture. In a rectangular baking dish, lay the brioche slices, pour the egg mixture over, and let soak for 10 minutes. Drain off the excess egg mixture and discard it. In a cast-iron skillet over medium heat, melt the 2 teaspoons of the reserved bacon fat. Once the fat is hot, grill the soaked brioche to a golden brown on both sides, about 5 minutes.

To serve, put a piece of brioche in the center of a dessert plate and top with about 3 tablespoons of the apple-bacon confit. Spoon some of the confit liquid onto the plate and add a scoop of vanilla ice cream. Top each plate with 1 slice of bacon candy.

NOTE: *This tasty little dessert is packed with all the flavors you think of on a chilly night, plus the crispy, smoky texture of bacon. Serve it with a hot mulled cider or a little Calavados.*

CHOCOLATE-DIPPED SMOKED ALMOND–BACON BRITTLE

Makes 3 pounds

¼ pound bacon

2 cups smoked almonds

1¼ cups sugar

¼ cup plus 2 tablespoons light corn syrup

¼ cup plus 2 tablespoons water

1 cup (2 sticks) unsalted butter, cut into ½-inch cubes, at room temperature

½ teaspoon baking soda

¼ teaspoon salt

½ teaspoon crushed pink peppercorns

8 ounces 60% cacao chocolate, chopped

Cut the bacon into bite-size pieces. Place the pieces in a large sauté pan and cook over medium heat until crispy, about 10 minutes. Drain and set aside. Coarsely chop the smoked almonds and set aside. Line a baking sheet with a Silpat liner or waxed paper.

In a large saucepan, combine the sugar, corn syrup, and water. Cook this mixture on medium-high heat for about 4 minutes, or until the sugar turns thick and syrupy. Slowly add the softened butter and continue stirring until the the mixture emulsifies. Keep cooking and stirring until mixture is golden brown, about 4 minutes longer. Remove the pan from the heat. If the mixture is not smooth,

whisk until it is smooth. Stir in the baking soda, salt, peppercorns, crispy bacon bits, and almonds. Quickly but carefully pour the brittle onto the prepared baking sheet. When cool and hard, break the brittle into bite-size pieces.

Melt the chocolate in the microwave in a microwave-safe bowl in 30-second intervals, stirring in between intervals, until the mixture is entirely melted but not hot. Cool the chocolate to room temperature, then either dip the pieces of brittle in the chocolate or drizzle the chocolate on top. Chill the brittle until the chocolate is set. Store in a tightly sealed container for up to 1 week.

BACORN (BACON-CARAMEL POPCORN WITH CHILE-SPIKED PEANUTS)

Makes 8 quarts

3 tablespoons corn oil

1⅓ cups popcorn kernels

Sea salt

1 cup crumbled cooked bacon

1 cup coarsely chopped roasted peanuts

Red chili powder

1 cup (2 sticks) butter

2 cups loosely packed brown sugar

½ cup honey

1 teaspoon baking soda

Coat the bottom of a large stockpot with the corn oil and add the popcorn kernels. Place the lid on the pot and cook over high heat, shaking the pot vigorously, until the popping slows almost to a stop. Remove the pot from the heat at once and empty the popped corn into 2 foil baking trays (the type hotels use, with 4- to 5-inch sides). Add salt to taste.

Sprinkle the crumbled bacon evenly over the popcorn in the two trays. Toss the chopped roasted peanuts in a small bowl with the red chili powder and salt to your desired heat level and sprinkle over the popcorn mixture. Set aside.

Preheat the oven to 250°F.

Melt the butter, brown sugar, honey, and a teaspoon or so of sea salt in a large saucepan over medium heat. Cook, stirring occasionally with a heatproof spatula, until the temperature reaches 250°F on a candy thermometer, which is the firm ball stage. Stir in the baking soda. The sauce will become lighter in color and foam up. When the baking soda is incorporated, pour the mixture evenly over the popcorn mixture and use heatproof spatulas to toss to coat.

Bake for about 20 minutes, then remove the pans from the oven, mix with a heatproof spatula, and return the pans to the oven for 10 to 15 minutes until caramelized. Remove the caramel corn from the oven and spread it on baking sheets to cool. When cool, break up the clumps with your hands and serve.

CHOCOLATE-BACON CUPCAKES

Makes 12

MAPLE–BROWN BUTTER–BACON FROSTING

8 slices ¼-inch-thick bacon, diced into ¼-inch pieces

1 cup (2 sticks) butter

¼ cup milk

¼ cup heavy whipping cream

2 tablespoons crème fraîche

1 tablespoon vanilla extract

3 tablespoons maple syrup

1 teaspoon salt

3 cups confectioners' sugar

CUPCAKES

8 tablespoons (1 stick) unsalted butter, at room temperature, plus more for the pan

1 cup cake flour or all-purpose flour

2 tablespoons unsweetened cocoa powder

½ teaspoon baking powder

½ teaspoon baking soda

1 teaspoon ground cinnamon

½ cup granulated sugar

¾ cup packed light brown sugar

½ teaspoon salt

2 large eggs

½ cup buttermilk, at room temperature

3 ounces bittersweet chocolate, chopped

3 tablespoons old-fashioned oats

1 teaspoon Maldon sea salt (see Notes)

To make the frosting, in a large sauté pan over medium heat, cook the bacon until crispy, about 10 minutes. Using a mesh sieve, drain the bacon bits by pouring the rendered bacon fat into the bowl of a mixer. Set the bacon pieces aside.

In the same sauté pan, melt the butter and cook until it turns brown and gives off a nutty fragrance, scraping the bottom of the pan occasionally so the butter doesn't burn. When the butter is dark and begins to burn, immediately remove the pan from the heat, scrape all of the browned bits loose, and transfer the contents to the mixing bowl with the bacon fat. Refrigerate the bowl until the butter is cold. Meanwhile, in a separate bowl, mix together the milk, cream, crème fraîche, vanilla, and maple syrup; set aside.

Fit your electric mixer with the paddle attachment. When the browned butter is cold, cream it on medium speed with the salt until blended. Add the confectioners' sugar and continue to cream at medium speed until fluffy, about 8 minutes. Slowly add the milk mixture and continue mixing until smooth and homogeneous. Refrigerate until cold.

Preheat the oven to 350°F. Lightly butter a standard 12-cup muffin pan, or line it with cupcake liners, and set aside.

To make the cupcakes, sift together the flour, cocoa powder, baking powder, baking soda, and cinnamon in a medium bowl. Put the ½ cup of butter, the sugars, and salt into the bowl of an electric mixer fitted with the paddle attachment. Cream on medium speed until the mixture is light and fluffy, about 5 minutes. With the machine running, add the eggs, one at a time, and mix until well incorporated, about 2 minutes.

Scrape down the sides and bottom of the bowl, turn the speed to low, and add one-quarter of the dry ingredient mixture. When no traces of flour remain, add one-third of the buttermilk and mix until incorporated. Continue evenly alternating the flour mixture and the buttermilk, ending with the flour mixture. Scrape down the sides and bottom of the bowl and mix in the chopped chocolate and oatmeal. Divide the batter between the 12 muffin cups; each cup should be three-quarters full. Bake until a tester inserted in the center comes out clean, about 30 minutes. Remove the cupcakes from the muffin tin and cool completely on a rack.

When the cupcakes are completely cool, fluff the cold frosting with a small offset spatula until soft and spreadable but not runny. Place about 3 tablespoons of frosting on top of each cupcake, then sprinkle on about ½ teaspoon of bacon bits and a pinch of Maldon salt. Serve immediately. Or if you prefer, you can refrigerate the cupcakes until the frosting is firm.

NOTES: *This cupcake is based upon several breakfast flavors: butter, maple, vanilla, cinnamon, egg, oatmeal, chocolate, and bacon. Bacon provides crunch, and the savory quality it adds is surprisingly appealing in contrast to the bittersweet and creaminess of chocolate. The burnt bits of the bacon and brown butter also add a deep caramel flavor to the soft textured and light cake. The saltiness of the Maldon salt in the icing makes your mouth water at first taste, increasing your sensory experience to the spices and flavors of the cupcakes.*

Maldon salt is a type of delicate, flaky sea salt produced in England. It can be purchased in some specialty stores and online.

CANE SUGAR AND BACON-ICED CUPCAKES

Makes 12

CANDIED BACON

2 cups diced bacon (preferably Benton's smoked country bacon)

4 large egg whites

1 cup granulated sugar

VANILLA PASTRY CREAM FILLING

2 quarts milk

4 cups granulated sugar

4 vanilla beans

3¼ cups all-purpose flour

24 large egg yolks

CUPCAKES

1 cup (2 sticks) unsalted butter

¾ cup granulated sugar

4 large eggs

2⅔ cups sifted all-purpose flour

2¼ teaspoons baking powder

½ teaspoon salt

1 cup whole milk

1½ teaspoons vanilla extract

4 large egg whites

ICING

4 tablespoons (½ stick) unsalted butter, at room temperature

2 cups sifted confectioners' sugar

1 teaspoon vanilla extract

¼ teaspoon salt

2 tablespoons Steen's cane syrup

Preheat the oven to 325ºF. Line a baking sheet with a Silpat mat or parchment paper. Line a standard 12-cup muffin pan with paper liners.

To make the candied bacon, cook the bacon in a large skillet over medium heat until semi-crunchy, about 10 minutes. Drain on paper towels. Place the egg whites and sugar in a large bowl and whisk until the egg whites begin to foam heavily. Fold the bacon into the mixture. Transfer it to the baking sheet and bake for 15 to 20 minutes, or until the bacon is crispy. Once the bacon is out of the oven, you may want to sprinkle on a little more sugar to give it a bit of texture. Set the candied bacon aside.

To make the vanilla pastry cream filling, place the milk, sugar, and vanilla beans in a large pot over medium heat and bring it to 220°F on a candy thermometer. In a large bowl, combine the flour and egg yolks. Slowly add the warm milk mixture to the egg mixture to temper it, and then transfer the mixture back into the pot. Bring the whole mixture to a boil slowly over medium heat while stirring constantly to avoid scorching the bottom.

The mixture will thicken after a few minutes. Once thickened, remove the pan from the heat and chill the mixture until ready to use.

To make the cupcakes, combine the butter and ½ cup of the sugar in the large bowl of an electric mixer fitted with the paddle attachment and beat until incorporated, 2 to 3 minutes. Add the eggs one at a time, beating after each addition, and mix until fully incorporated and smooth. In a separate bowl, combine the flour, baking powder, and salt. Begin to add the flour mixture to the mixer bowl one-quarter at a time, alternating with the milk and vanilla until all the flour and milk have been added, ending with the flour. Transfer the batter to another large bowl.

Fit your electric mixer with the whisk attachment. Place the egg whites in a large mixing bowl and whip, slowly adding the remaining ¼ cup sugar, until a stiff meringue forms. Use a spatula to slowly fold the meringue into the cupcake batter in 4 batches, folding just until each batch is fully incorporated.

Divide the batter equally among the prepared muffin cups and bake for 15 minutes, or until a toothpick inserted in the center of a cupcake comes out clean. Cool the cupcakes to room temperature. At this point, the cupcakes can be wrapped in plastic or stored in an airtight container and frozen for up to 2 weeks.

To make the icing, combine the butter, confectioners' sugar, vanilla, and salt in an electric mixer fitted with the paddle attachment. Mix until incorporated, then slowly add the cane syrup. Transfer the icing to a piping bag fitted with a star tip.

To assemble the cupcakes, use a melon baller or small spoon to core out the center of each cupcake. Start from the top of the cupcake and slowly remove a good amount from the center. Do not puncture the bottom of the cupcake. Fill the center of each cupcake to the top with the chilled vanilla pastry cream, but do not overfill. Pipe the icing on top and garnish with the candied bacon.

BACON PANNA COTTA WITH HUCKLEBERRIES

Serves 4

¼ pound sliced bacon

4 cups heavy whipping cream

1 cup plus 1 teaspoon granulated sugar

4½ teaspoons unflavored gelatin powder

Salt and black pepper

4 ounces wild huckleberries or blueberries (optional; see Note)

Celery leaves, for garnish (optional)

Preheat the oven to 350°F. Cut the bacon into small pieces, place them in an ovenproof skillet, and roast until brown, about 10 minutes. Drain off the bacon fat and reserve it, then add the heavy cream to the pan, bring it to a boil, then turn off the heat, and cover the pan with a lid. Let it rest for 30 minutes, then strain the bacon out of the heavy cream, leaving the cream in the pan. Reserve the bacon.

Heat the heavy cream over medium heat, add the sugar and gelatin, and season with salt and black pepper. Spray 4 (2-ounce) bowls with nonstick cooking spray, pour the cream mixture into the bowls, and chill until set.

Unmold each panna cotta onto a serving plate. Heat the reserved bacon fat, add the huckleberries, and crush them while stirring. Cool the mixture a bit. Serve the panna cotta topped with huckleberry sauce and garnished with celery leaves and the reserved bacon pieces.

NOTE: *Huckleberries are small and round, usually less than ¼ inch in diameter, and contain about 10 relatively large seeds. The berries range in color from bright red, to dark purple, and blue depending on the variety. In taste, the berries range from tart to sweet, with a flavor similar to that of a blueberry, especially in blue- and purple-colored varieties.*

CHEF CORY BARRETT, **LOLA, CLEVELAND, OHIO**

MAPLE-BACON ICE CREAM

Makes 2 quarts

3 ounces bacon, minced

4 cups whole milk

¼ cup nonfat dry milk

⅓ cup heavy whipping cream

¼ cup granulated sugar

12 large egg yolks

2½ cups maple syrup

Place the bacon pieces in a large skillet and cook over medium heat until crispy. Drain and cool on paper towels.

Fill a large bowl halfway with ice and water and set it aside.

Combine the whole milk, dry milk, and cream in a large saucepan and bring to a boil over medium heat. Remove from the heat and set aside. Combine the sugar and egg yolks in a large bowl and mix well. Slowly add the hot cream to this egg mixture in small portions to temper it, stirring constantly and being careful not to scramble the eggs.

Return the mixture to the saucepan and cook over medium heat, stirring constantly, until the mixture is thick enough to coat the back of a wooden spoon. Remove the pan from the heat and chill it over the ice water bath for about 30 minutes. Once cooled, stir in the maple syrup.

Pour the mixture into an ice-cream maker and churn according to the manufacturer's instructions. When the ice cream is fully churned, scoop it into a freezer-safe container and stir in the bacon pieces. Freeze until ready to serve.

CAT CORA, IRON CHEF; OWNER, **KOUZZINA, ORLANDO, FLORIDA**

PIG CANDY ICE CREAM

Makes 1½ quarts

1 pound applewood-smoked bacon	3 cups heavy whipping cream	1¼ cups granulated sugar
½ cup loosely packed dark brown sugar	1 cup milk	4 large egg yolks
	1 vanilla bean, split	

Preheat the oven to 400°F. Lay the bacon on a baking sheet, sprinkle the brown sugar on top, and bake for 14 to16 minutes, until crispy. Cool the bacon, then finely chop it.

Combine the cream, milk, vanilla bean, and granulated sugar in a large saucepan and cook over medium-high heat until hot and the sugar is completely dissolved, stirring occasionally, about 5 minutes. Remove the vanilla bean and discard it.

In a small bowl, beat the egg yolks until smooth. Slowly whisk in 1 cup of the hot cream mixture. Return the yolk mixture to the saucepan and cook over medium heat, stirring continuously, until the mixture is thick enough to coat the back of a wooden spoon, 6 to 8 minutes. Do not let it boil.

Strain the mixture into a clean bowl and let it cool completely. Stir in the bacon bits. Pour the mixture into an ice-cream maker and freeze according to the manufacturer's instructions. When the ice cream is fully churned, scoop it into a freezer-safe container and freeze until ready to serve.

CONTRIBUTORS' BIOGRAPHIES

RODELIO AGLIBOT

Rodelio Aglibot grew up on both sides of the Pacific Rim and began studying and working in the culinary world at a young age. He was involved in five restaurant openings in San Francisco over a span of three years, most notably the E & O Trading Company, a Pan-Asian restaurant under the direction of chefs Joyce Goldstein and Gary Woo. As the opening sous chef, he furthered his education in Asian cuisine and began to hone his own culinary identity. Rodelio credits Joyce Goldstein and the late Barbara Tropp as influential chefs who imparted wisdom and confidence. He then became the opening executive chef and consultant of ZaZen in Venice, California. A few years later he became the executive chef of Koi Restaurant in Los Angeles, where he earned his stars for creating an innovative menu of Asian dishes. Aglibot established himself as a respected and personable chef, focusing on traditional Japanese ingredients with an essence of French technique and Californian style. Within two years of being at the helm at Koi, Rodelio had an opportunity to develop his own concept leading to the creation of the restaurant Yi Cuisine, which went on to be named one of the "Best New Asian Restaurants" by *Food & Wine* magazine.

In 2007, at a Meals-on-Wheels fundraiser in Chicago, Aglibot met Chef James Gottwald, the director of culinary operations for Chicago's Rockit Ranch Productions, and Sunda was born. He is now executive chef and continues as a consulting chef. He is also involved in several ventures supplying the freshest ingredients most notably tuna to chefs in the United States. He is known as "the Food Buddha," because of his dedication to his heritage and his approach to menu development.

MARK ALLEN

A native of Massachusetts, Mark Allen began his culinary training at age fifteen and is a graduate of the Culinary Institute of America. Mark is recognized both locally and nationally and has been featured on the Television Food Network, local Boston radio stations, and in a variety of local and national publications. He has graced professional kitchens across America with his culinary talents and traveled far and wide as a chef, from Little Dix Bay in Virgin Gorda, British Virgin Islands, to Arizona, where he worked under Chef Alessandro Strata's Mobil five-star restaurant at The Phoenician Resort, and to The Opera in San Francisco. In 1997 Mark took the opportunity to return to his hometown, where he was appointed chef of The Dining Room at The Ritz-Carlton. There, he was responsible for the culinary development, execution, presentation, and menu preparation for the restaurant. He was the youngest and only American chef to head the award-winning Dining Room. Mark Allen has been back in Boston for five years now, and has recently opened his own restaurant, Le Soir, which marries contemporary French cuisine with neighborhood appeal.

CORY BARRETT

Cory Barrett has been creating exciting finales for over a decade, and is now doing so behind the stoves of Michael Symon's James Beard Foundation Award–winning Lola Restaurant. No stranger to the fine dining scene, Cory honed his craft at the highly regarded Tribute Restaurant in Detroit, working alongside award-winning chef Takashi Yagihashi. Prior to taking the pastry helm at Lola, he opened Okada restaurant at the five-star Wynn resort in Las Vegas, skillfully blending Japanese flavors and modern pastry techniques. With such depth of culinary diversity his rule-breaking desserts show no limits and will dazzle for decades to come.

MICHELLE BERNSTEIN

Since the pivotal Mango Gang era in the late '80s and early '90s, no other Miami chef has made as big a splash on the national culinary scene as Chef Michelle Bernstein has. A Miami native of Jewish and Latin descent, this passionate chef has dazzled diners and critics alike with her sublime cuisine and a personality as bright and vibrant as the Florida sun. "My food is luxurious but approachable," says Bernstein, a James Beard Foundation Award winner (Best Chef: South, 2008)

and author of *Cuisine à Latina* (Houghton Mifflin Harcourt, 2008). "You don't need heavy-handed techniques and over-the-top presentations to make a dish work. It's about amazing ingredients, layered flavors, and simplicity. I cook the food I love and I think that love translates to the diners." Right now, diners love Bernstein's cuisine at her two successful Miami outposts, Michy's and Sra. Martinez, which she owns and operates with her husband and partner, David Martinez. Sporting distinctly different styles and cuisines, both restaurants display the earnestness, passion, and dedication that have made Bernstein one of the region's brightest culinary stars. In addition to an ever-growing restaurant empire—Michelle Bernstein at The Omphoy in Palm Beach County, Florida, opened in the fall of 2009—Bernstein recently launched the Miami chapter of Common Threads, an after-school program dedicated to teaching underprivileged kids ages eight to eleven to cook, socialize, and eat healthy.

JASON BERTHOLD

Jason Berthold's style of cuisine is equal parts modern and disciplined. It is cleanly rooted in classic training, though not constrained by predisposed limitations or boundaries. Berthold thrives on delivering pure, vibrant flavors that showcase each ingredient with equal enthusiasm and respect. He revels in the process, the transformation of the raw ingredient to its final destination, which is akin to the journey of grape to glass in winemaking. As winemaker for his own label, Courier, Berthold strives for a balanced dance between the plate and the glass. Given the creative freedom to develop his own menu at RN74, Berthold takes a modern, yet simple approach to regional French fare, while positioning wine pairing as a vital slice of the dining experience. In tandem with his entree into culinary fortitude at French Laundry, Berthold was entranced by Napa Valley and the rhythms of winemaking. The physical, hands-on worlds of kitchen and cellar became surprisingly similar to him. "In both worlds," said Berthold, "decisions are based on the senses—taste, sight, smell, and the memory of those senses are what fuel winemakers and chefs alike."

JOHN BESH

In the early fall of 2009, chef John Besh effectively doubled the size of his restaurant family by opening Domenica, a contemporary Italian trattoria, and the nostalgic, playful concept of the American Sector, in the World War II museum. These join his restaurant August, which highlights the finest of dining with the flair of local ingredients and has twice been listed on *Gourmet* magazine's list of Best Restaurants; Besh Steak, the chef's creative interpretation of the all-American steakhouse with a nod to New Orleans cuisine; the venerable La Provence, which is a return to John's personal history, with a farm that generates both livestock and produce for the restaurants; and Lüke, a long-held dream that pays homage to the old brasseries that once reigned in New Orleans with its French and German influences. In 2009 Besh celebrated his life growing up in Louisiana in *My New Orleans: The Cookbook*. It's a beautiful cookbook and memoir of his culinary journey through the traditions and culture of this great southern state. A recipient of

the James Beard Award for Best Chef: Southeast, Besh is the spokesman for the Louisiana Seafood Council and a member of the Southern Foodways Alliance and an advocate for bettering the life of individuals in the hospitality industry.

RICHARD BETTS

Richard Betts is a former geologist and award-winning sommelier while at the Little Nell in Aspen, Colorado. He is now co-owner and winemaker of Betts and Scholl, as well as cofounder of Sombra Mezcal with partners Dennis Scholl and Charles Beiler.

BLACK ROCK SPIRITS

Black Rock Spirits was officially launched in 2008 by three friends: Chris Marshall, Stefan Schachtell, and Sven Liden. They started testing with bacon infusions a few years ago and decided that it was so good in a Bloody Mary they wanted to make it a commercial product. In April of 2009, the first bottle of BAKON vodka, a delicious pepper bacon–flavored potato-based vodka, hit the shelves. Taste tests with Bloody Marys using BAKON vodka comparing it to other high-end vodkas almost felt like cheating—like adding bacon to a recipe at a cook-off contest! Bartenders have come up with some really interesting (and tasty) drinks, from the Hawaiian Luau to the Chocolate Bakon Martini. It's an ingredient not commonly found behind most bars, so interest ranges from high-end lounges that mix it with smoky scotch and blue cheese stuffed olives, to college bars that are trying to come up with the perfect "bacon bomb," to the trendy speakeasy that stirs it with orange liqueurs and bitters looking to concoct a complex cocktail. Visit www.bakonvodka.com for more information.

SEAN BRASEL

Behind every great restaurant, there's a creative and talented chef who brings passion, dedication, and excellence to every bite; Colorado-born chef Sean Brasel (age thirty-nine) is such a chef. Working with business partner David Tornek for twelve years, Brasel has created the tastiest menus and hottest see-and-be-seen restaurant concepts in the business. Their latest creation, Meat Market, a sizzling contemporary American steakhouse with a New York City vibe located at 915 Lincoln Road in the heart of South Beach, has taken the city and restaurant critics by storm. Brasel's menu embraces the staples of a classic steakhouse, a variety of prime cuts, generous portions of innovative seafood, amazing sides, and appetizers—and infuses them with an artful, contemporary spin, appealing to those looking for a traditional experience as well as those who are more adventurous. A graduate of the prestigious Madeline Kamman's School for American Chefs in Napa Valley, Brasel met Tornek in 1994 when they opened several successful restaurants in Colorado, before relocating to South Florida to launch Touch on Lincoln Road. A precursor to Meat Market, Touch garnered acclaim for Brasel's ambitious contemporary American cuisine, and Brasel became a go-to talent for off-site catering, eventually leading to the creation of Touch Catering in 2005, a wildly successful venture from the get go, drawing big name clients and positioning Chef Brasel as a superstar on South Florida's catering circuit. For more information, visit www.meatmarketmiami.com.

SAUL BOLTON

Saul Bolton has spent the past ten years refining his namesake restaurant, SAUL, in the Boerum Hill neighborhood of Brooklyn, New York. SAUL has garnered four consecutive Michelin stars and ranks in Zagat's top fifty New York restaurants. Recently Saul opened The Vanderbilt in Prospect Heights, Brooklyn.

RYAN BUTLER

As executive pastry chef at Double Crown and Madam Geneva in New York, Ryan Butler's elegant desserts deftly combine the perfume and spice of Asia with traditional British favorites. A native of Carmel, New York, Chef Butler received a degree in Pastry Arts from the Culinary Institute of America, and began his professional career at Park Avenue Café, becoming sous chef to his mentor, Richard Leach. Chef Butler went on to develop his unique combination of neoclassic and modern techniques and his savory approach to pastry as head pastry chef at Tocqueville Restaurant, the Gramercy Park Hotel, and as executive pastry chef at Django Restaurant.

MONICA BYRNE

Monica Byrne is the chef of Home/Made Wine Bar and Roquette Catering, both based in Red Hook, Brooklyn, New York. For more information, visit www.homemadebklyn.com or www.roquettecatering.com.

IAN CHALERMKITTICHAI

Chef Chalermkittichai is Thailand's first international celebrity chef. With a weekly cooking television show, *Chef Mue Thong (Golden Hand Chef)*, which can be seen in over fifty countries around the world, his audience is truly global. Chef Chalermkittichai created the celebrated New York City Kittichai Restaurant in 2004. In 2008 he left to form his global food and beverage management and consulting firm, Cuisine Concept Co., Ltd., through which he created Murmuri in Barcelona, I Sea Restaurant in Hua Hin, and Hyde & Seek Gastro Bar in Bangkok. He also advises over twenty clients worldwide. Next up on Chef Chalermkittichai's horizon is a signature Thai restaurant in Mumbai, a signature Thai restaurant in Paris, and a signature fine dining restaurant in Bangkok. Keep up with the chef via his Web site: www.ianchalermkittichai.com.

DAVID COLEMAN

Formerly the executive chef at Union Pacific, Atlas, and then Duvet, David Coleman is now the chef de cuisine at Tocqueville Restaurant in New York City.

CAT CORA

In 2005, Cat made television history on the Food Network's *Iron Chef America* as the first and only female Iron Chef, and in November 2006 *Bon Appétit* magazine bestowed her with their Teacher of the Year Award. She is the author of two cookbooks, *Cat Cora's Kitchen* and *Cooking from the Hip: Fast, Easy, Phenomenal Meals*. A busy mom of four young boys, Cat recently celebrated the opening of her first sit-down restaurant Kouzzina (Greek for "kitchen") by Cat Cora at Walt Disney World's Boardwalk Resort in Orlando, Florida.

CHRIS COSENTINO

Chris Cosentino is the executive chef of San Francisco's Incanto and cocreator of Boccalone, an artisanal salumeria. Cosentino is nationally acclaimed as a leading proponent of offal cookery and head-to-tail cuisine, and his approach is marked by sheer gusto, careful research, precise technique, and a belief that no parts of an animal slaughtered for food should go to waste. At Incanto, his innovative interpretations of rustic Italian fare have garnered critical praise and an avid following, while his abiding passion for offal has led him to work on the definitive cookbook on the subject, aimed at providing essential instruction on the preparation of offal for both professional and home cooks.

NATHAN CRAVE

Nathan Crave is originally from upstate New York and as a teenager relocated to the Pacific Northwest, where he graduated from the Culinary Arts Program at North Seattle Community College. After graduation, Nathan worked with celebrated Seattle chefs Tom Douglas and Eric Tanaka of the Dahlia Lounge, and later in Boston with Michael Schlow and Patrick Connolly of Radius, Stephan Sherman of Union, and Gabriel Frasca of Spire. Upon his return to Seattle, Nathan worked as the sous chef at Spring Hill restaurant alongside chef/owner Mark Fuller before taking on the executive chef role with Monsoon restaurants.

ANDREA CURTO-RANDAZZO

Talula, which opened in the heart of Miami Beach's arts district in June 2003, and Creative Tastes Catering, launched in October 2007, are the brainchildren of Andrea Curto-Randazzo and husband-chef Frank Randazzo. Originally from Vero Beach, Florida, Andrea was raised in an Italian family and claims that her grandmother was "the best cook ever," citing her as a direct influence on her decision to pursue a career in the culinary arts. After waiting tables to make ends meet and attending the Culinary Institute of America, where she graduated with honors, Curto-Randazzo took up residence at New York's Tribeca Grill under Don Pintabona. It was while working there that she met Frank, her future husband and business partner. Looking to fine-tune her skills, she left Tribeca Grill to work at Aja, under Chef Gary Robbins. In 1996, Curto-Randazzo returned to South Florida and accepted a job as the pastry and sous chef at The Heights. When Curto-Randazzo departed from Wish as executive sous chef, she and Frank opened Talula. Serving eclectic American cuisine in an environment that is equal parts haute haunt and comfy neighborhood restaurant, Talula has been heralded by the *New York Times*, *Bon Appétit*, *Food & Wine*, and *Gourmet*. Encompassing flavors from the Caribbean, Asia, Latin America, Italy, and America, Talula's cuisine is a unique blend of the Randazzos' shared influences, tastes, and culinary approaches.

MICAH EDELSTEIN

Micah Edelstein is the proprietress and menu guru behind The Wandering Chef Caterers, a go-anywhere-their-clients-need-them gourmet service, and the new executive chef at Grass Restaurant & Lounge in the fashionable Design District of Miami. The restaurant features her world-renowned Eclectic World Cuisine.

COLBY GARRELTS

Chef Colby Garrelts, who has been nominated in 2010, 2009, 2008, and 2007 for Best Chef: Midwest by the James Beard Foundation and was named as one of the Top 10 Best New Chefs in 2005 by *Food & Wine* magazine, obtained his culinary education in kitchens across the country. At TRU, Garrelts honed his technical skills, developed his culinary style, and met his wife and partner, Megan Schultz. A native of Kansas, Colby married Megan and returned to Kansas City, Missouri, in 2003. The couple located a building in the heart of Westport, Kansas City's entertainment district, and opened Blue Stem on March 15, 2004. The restaurant has received rave reviews, including 2007 *Santé Magazine* Restaurant of the Year, a four-star rating from *Kansas City Magazine*, and *Wine Spectator*'s prestigious Award of Excellence. Insisting on "his way," chef Colby Garrelts has successfully shown that this can result in an exceptional restaurant and award-winning cuisine!

JACQUES GAUTIER

Chef Jacques Gautier's restaurant Palo Santo operates out of the ground floor of a Brooklyn brownstone. His eclectic take on traditional Latin American cuisine draws influence from Caribbean family roots. In 1998 he completed the chef training program at The Natural Gourmet Institute. At age twenty, Chef Gautier was invited to cook at the

James Beard House, and he remains the youngest person to have received that honor. Before opening his own restaurants, he worked in the renowned kitchens of Vong in New York and Azie in San Francisco. Gautier spent most of 2004 traveling and working as a winemaker's assistant in Argentina. During his travels, he conducted an intensive study of South American wine and perfected the Latin market cooking that Palo Santo offers on a daily changing menu.

RYAN HARDY

Chef Hardy summarizes his cooking style with a simple, "I love to handcraft food." A true artisan, Chef Hardy cures his own prosciutto, preserves and pickles every fruit, vegetable, and meat in season, and even makes his own raw milk cheeses. Since joining Aspen's premier hotel, the Little Nell, in 2005, Chef Hardy has been providing the exclusive mountain town with his signature Italian farmhouse cooking. In 2007, he started Rendezvous Organic Farm, a twenty-five-acre former bed and breakfast, to raise the foods of his Kentucky roots exclusively for Montagna and Ajax Tavern, the two restaurants within the Little Nell. He has twice been nominated a James Beard Best Chef Finalist, and he was named Best New Chef in New England by *Yankee Magazine*.

GARETH HUGHES

Gareth Hughes is a Liverpool-born, New Zealand–reared Brooklynite. He holds a master's degree in psychology and a New York City yellow cab driver's license, and he managed a Disaster Assistance Center in Manhattan in the aftermath of 9/11.

Gareth spent more years than could possibly be healthy as a bartender and later sold his soul for a green card (by working for a corporate, people-consuming machine—a staffing agency) before deciding to make it up to the world by following his passion: authentic Down Under–style meat and vegetarian pies. Down Under Bakery (DUB) Pies was born in New York City in 2003, and seven years later is actually threatening to show a profit. DUB Pies is singularly about perfecting the gestalt of a great meat pie—awesome flaky pastry and consistently high-quality ingredients that make memorable fillings. Well, that and a bloody good coffee in the form of the phenomenon that is the Flat White. See what he means at www.dubpies.com.

ANDY HUSBANDS

Andy Husbands is the award-winning chef/owner of Tremont 647 and Sister Sorel, located in Boston's South End. Raised in Seattle, Husbands makes his home in Boston, and has been a major player in Boston's culinary scene for over fifteen years. Also known as "The Fearless Chef," Husbands has published a cookbook by the same name and is well known by his peers both locally and nationally for his bold cooking style, extensive charity work with leading hunger-relief organization Share Our Strength, and his endeavors on the competitive barbecue circuit. Most notably, Husbands's team took first place in the Jack Daniel's World Championship Invitational Barbecue in Lynchburg, Tennessee, and first place in the brisket category in 2007 at the American Royal Barbecue. Husbands also appeared on season six of the FOX Television Network's series *Hell's Kitchen*, with Chef Gordon

Ramsey. His goal is simple: teaching and making his signature flavors of bold American cuisine with adventurous global influences accessible to all. He can be found by blog, on Twitter, and Facebook, as well as on his first-of-its-kind Kitchen Cam, an online live feed from Tremont 647's kitchen.

RHONDA KAVE

Rhonda Kave, an entrepreneur and chocolatier, owns and operates Roni-Sue's Chocolates in the historic Essex Street Market on New York City's Lower East Side. Noted for her "fiendish" Pig Candy, Kave also makes over thirty varieties of hand-rolled and dipped truffles, tea and honey lollipops, and signature candy buttercrunch in her open production kitchen in the market. Roni-Sue's Chocolates are also available online at www.roni-sue.com and at fine gourmet shops such as Dean & DeLuca nationwide.

BOB KINKEAD

Bob Kinkead is the chef and owner of Kinkead's in Washington, D.C., Hell Point Seafood in Annapolis, Maryland, and co-owner of Sibling Rivalry in Boston with his brother David. He has worked in the restaurant business for over thirty-eight years and is the recipient of the James Beard Foundation, Ivy, Silver Plate, and Fine Dining Hall of Fame awards, among others. Bob resides with his wife, Dianne, in Great Falls, Virginia.

CHRISTOPHER KRONNER

As executive chef of Bar Tartine, Kronner maintains a progressive yet classic approach to cooking. His longstanding relationship with owners Elisabeth Prueitt and Chad Robertson makes for a homecoming of sorts; as a recent transplant to San Francisco, Kronner once worked at Tartine Bakery (staying in the apartment upstairs) and took inspiration and guidance from its founders. Bar Tartine's menu is a collaboration among Kronner, Prueitt, and Robertson, blending traditional European dishes and contemporary Bay Area influences. "Using things from people that I have personal relationships with matters so much to me," he explains. Whether it's the rancher, farmer, or bread baker, Kronner is guided the old-fashioned way, not only by the ingredients but also by their makers.

ANITA LO

A Michigan-born, first-generation Chinese American, Anita Lo has never worked anywhere other than in the kitchen. To satisfy both her hunger for fine food and her desire to learn French, Anita went to Paris to study the art of cooking during the summer of her junior year. Immediately upon her graduation, she went to work in the garde-manger station of the year-old Bouley restaurant. That year whetted Anita's appetite and she returned to France to earn her degree in cooking at the prestigious Ritz-Escoffier school. Her work at Bouley paid off, and she graduated first in her class with honors. This earned her sought-after internships at several two-star Michelin-rated restaurants in Paris, under such noted chefs as Michel Rostang and Guy Savoy. In 2005, in the first season of *Iron Chef America*, she defeated Iron Chef Mario Batali with the first all-female challenger team. Still, Anita's appetite was not sated. After two years she left her position at

Mirezi to travel the world with her partner, Jennifer. Annisa opened in June of 2000 to a glowing two-star review from Bill Grimes of the *New York Times*. She was named Best New Restaurant Chef by the *Village Voice* that same year. In 2001, she received the highly coveted Best New Chef award from *Food & Wine* Magazine. In 2002, she was named one of nine Culinary Wizards in *New York Magazine*'s first annual food awards. In 2004, Women Chefs and Restaurateurs awarded her with the Golden Whisk award at their Women Who Inspire ceremony, and in 2005, she won a *New York Moves* magazine Women of Power award. She has maintained a Michelin star in all of the guide's yearly New York City publications and a "27" food rating in the populist Zagat guide. In 2007, she was voted one of the one hundred most influential women in business by Crains' New York. In 2005, Rickshaw Dumpling Bar, a quick casual Asian concept where Anita is chef and partner, opened. She continues to work on helping to make Rickshaw a national chain.

ZARELA MARTINEZ

Born in the Sonoran border town of Agua Prieta, Zarela Martinez is a renowned cultural interpreter between Mexico and the United States through the medium of food. Since 1987 her eponymous restaurant Zarela has set standards of authenticity on the New York culinary scene with weekly gastronomic tours of different states that are exposing Manhattan diners to the richness and variety of Mexican cuisine. A sought-after speaker and consultant for major corporations, she also wrote the pioneering cookbooks *Food from My Heart*, *The Food and Life of Oaxaca*, and *Zarela's Veracruz*,

the last published in conjunction with her public television series *¡Zarela! La Cocina Veracruzana*. Her Web site www.zarela.com is an invaluable resource for lovers of Mexican food and culture, as are her entertaining and insightful how-to videos on basic Mexican cooking techniques and flavor principles, featured on www.youtube.com.

BILL MCDANIEL

As executive chef at the Red Cat in New York, Bill McDaniel is a long way from the days when he toiled as a short order cook as a teenager at Swenson's Ice Cream Factory in Tucson, Arizona. After years of cooking in kitchens across the country, Bill found the right one. At the Red Cat, he displays his signature style of "food people can relate to," which is straightforward and comfortable. He thinks people should be able to enjoy good times and good people wherever they go, and food plays a large role in that.

JULIAN MEDINA

Julian Medina has been creating refined Latin cuisine for nearly fifteen years. He trained professionally at Hacienda de Los Morales and Les Celebrites in Mexico, and then at New York City's French Culinary Institute where he received the Best Final Project award. Julian cooked at a number of top Latin restaurants, including Maya and Pampano, but truly came into his own when he opened his Mexican bistro Toloache in August 2007. Less than a year later, in June 2008, Julian opened Yerba Buena in Manhattan's East Village, a restaurant whose menu traverses Peru, Cuba, Argentina, Colombia, Mexico, and Spain. The success of Yerba Buena led Julian to open a second location in the West Village, Yerba Buena Perry. You can find information on all three restaurants at www.ybandco.com.

GEORGE MENDES

A first-generation American born to Portuguese parents, George has fond memories of the elaborate, festive meals his family would prepare while he was growing up in Danbury, Connecticut. Soon after finishing high school, Mendes enrolled in the Culinary Institute of America. After graduating in 1992, Mendes worked at the original Bouley in Tribeca, where he met his mentor, chef David Bouley. He also participated in two month-long stages at Alain Passard's Arpege in Paris, France. During his year and a half at Lespinasse, Mendes traveled to France and staged at Le Moulin de Mougins under the legendary Roger Vergé, and at La Bastide de Moustiers under Alain Ducasse. The Bastide menu, which changed daily, relied on the adjacent garden for all vegetables and herbs, and Mendes enjoyed working in an environment that emphasized the freshness and seasonality of the ingredients. He then returned to New York to help his friend and fellow Bouley alumnus Kurt Gutenbrunner open his Austrian restaurant, Wallsé. In 2003, Mendes staged with highly acclaimed Basque chef Martin Berasategui at his eponymous three-star Michelin restaurant in San Sebastián, Spain. There, he explored the heritage and contemporary culinary trends of the Iberian Peninsula. Upon returning to New York, he joined Tocqueville as chef de cuisine where he was inspired by the nearby greenmarket and his recent travels in Europe. After more than three years running the kitchen, Mendes left to pursue his own restaurant venture, Aldea.

WAYNE NISH

Wayne Nish began his culinary career at the Quilted Giraffe in 1984 and went on to helm La Colombe d'Or in 1988. He was the chef and owner of the acclaimed March Restaurant in New York City for seventeen years. Nish has earned twenty stars from the *New York Times*, won countless other awards during his career, was the first American to appear on *Iron Chef Japan*, and earned a Michelin star at March in 2006. He has worked and traveled extensively in Asia and is currently planning his next project in New York.

PICHET ONG

Pichet Ong is a New Yorker who grew up in Thailand, Hong Kong, and Singapore. Pichet was formerly the pastry chef at chef Jean-Georges Vongerichten's Spice Market and 66 and, prior to that, at Rick Moonan's RM. P*ONG was Pichet's first venture as both chef and owner. His first book, *the sweet spot*, was published in May 2007. Pichet has been consulting chef for Jean-Georges Vongerichten's 66 and Spice Market, where his desserts garnered him a three-star review in the *New York Times*. Despite Pichet's pedigree as a world-renowned pastry chef, the menu at P*ONG was decidedly savory, incorporating Pichet's genius for the innovative use of dessert techniques in savory cooking and his critically acclaimed ability to blur the line between sweet and savory. The result is a tantalizing and often surprising mix of flavors, textures, and temperatures. The menu at P*ONG was dynamic (often changing weekly) to reflect the availability of the freshest and highest quality seasonal ingredients. Pichet's cuisine also reflects the different cooking techniques and flavor profiles he experienced during his upbringing in Southeast Asia and his subsequent travels in Europe and the Far East. Pichet prefers to cook naturally and with a minimum of fuss, showcasing the simple but sophisticated marriage of a few key ingredients. As *O Magazine* put it, Pichet's cooking style is "elemental."

KEN ORINGER

Internationally renowned and award-winning chef Ken Oringer, the executive chef and co-owner of Clio Restaurant, has worked in some of the finest kitchens in the United States and around the world. Chef Oringer's penchant for experimentation as well as his ability to attain new thresholds of culinary creation created a unique niche on the culinary landscape.

ELIZABETH RAMSEY

After attending the Scottsdale Culinary Institute, Elizabeth Ramsey interned and stayed on for three years at Mary Elaine's at the Phoenician Resort in Scottsdale, Arizona. From there, she moved to the Royal Palms Resort and Spa and apprenticed under chocolate maestro Pierino Jermonti. She was Pastry Sous Chef for two years at the James Hotel in Scottsdale, and then worked for restaurant Fiamma for two years studying Italian pastries, becoming their executive pastry chef. The restaurant transformed into Asia de Cuba where

she learned the craft of both Asian and Cuban desserts. More recently she moved to Brooklyn and continued her study of chocolate at Jacques Torres, learning the ins and outs of large production chocolate and bonbon work. She is now the pastry chef at the Chocolate Room in Brooklyn, New York.

CHRISTOPHER RENDELL

Christopher Rendell has followed a steady path westward from his native Australia to the kitchen of New York's Double Crown and Madam Geneva, working with some of the most esteemed names in the restaurant industry along the way. Inspired by his love of the unlikely combination of efficiency and chaos in the kitchen, as well as by Marco Pierre White's iconic book, *White Heat*, Rendell has sought culinary knowledge high and low, from top kitchens to market stalls, in Asia, Europe, and the United States. At Double Crown, Rendell's wonderfully diverse repertoire of recipes and his particular affinity for British and Asian cuisine have garnered critical praise and a loyal following.

WILL SAVARESE

Will Savarese is the executive chef of Robert's Restaurant in the new "Score's New York." Twenty years ago, while attending St. John's University, Will got his start while working at La Côte Basque, where he learned his classical foundation of fine French cooking. After earning a business degree from St. John's University, Will enrolled at the Culinary Institute of America and worked at the River Café in Brooklyn, New York. Upon completing his culinary degree, Will went back to La Côte Basque, and then went on to work at Aureole and

Le Cirque. When La Côte Basque later reopened at a new location, Will returned as Chef de Cuisine. In 1995, it earned three stars from the *New York Times*. For many years, Will ran the kitchen of La Crémaillère in Bedford, New York, again earning three stars from the *New York Times*, May 26, 2002. Will opened a gastro pub called the Tap House in Tuckahoe, New York, and has again received three stars from the *New York Times*, March 16, 2008.

SANDRA STEFANI

Sandra Stefani, an accomplished and talented chef, arrived from Pisa, Italy, in 1979 and she has been hard at work in the kitchen since, evolving into the locally renowned chef she is today. Her latest venture, Casa Toscana Ristorante, is one of those rare jewels of neighborhood restaurants with two intimate dining rooms and an al fresco garden where diners can enjoy her homemade, unpretentious cooking, as well as an impressive wine collection with realistic prices all wrapped up in an authentic ambiance enough to transport you to Sandra's native Tuscany. A believer in good food and entertaining, Stefani teaches weekly hands-on cooking classes in her restaurant's kitchen for adults and children.

ALLEN SUSSER

Born in New York, Chef Allen has synthesized the essence of his adopted region of South Florida. Chef Allen's dramatic translation of the bounty of South Florida's foodstuffs became known as New World Cuisine, an innovative signature and important contribution to American culinary craftsmanship. In addition to Chef Allen's

restaurant in Aventura, Allen has written several books, publishes a monthly newsletter, and has created a number of gourmet products that are available on his Web site: www.chefallens.com.

BRADFORD THOMPSON

With a background deeply rooted in New England's culinary traditions, Connecticut-born Bradford Thompson spent his childhood summers in Maine with his grandparents developing a palette strongly influenced by the handpicked blueberries, fried clams, and fresh lobster rolls that surrounded him. Bradford's culinary evolution began while working alongside a butcher, where he developed skills vital to his cooking philosophies today. Other stops that shaped his path have included Lever House, Café Boulud, DANIEL, and executive chef of Mary Elaine's at the Phoenician in Scottsdale, Arizona. He has received such honors as one of *Food & Wine* magazine's Best New Chefs of 2004 and receiving the prestigious James Beard Foundation award for Best Chef: Southwest in 2006.

RICK TRAMONTO

Rick Tramonto is executive chef/partner at the world-renowned, four-star Relais & Chateaux restaurant Tru in Chicago. Tramonto is also culinary director of Tramonto's Steak & Seafood, RT Sushi Bar, and Osteria. He has received a bevy of awards and honors, including the James Beard Foundation award for Best Chef: Midwest; the Robert Mondavi Award for Culinary Excellence; *Food & Wine* magazine's Top 10 Best New Chefs 1994; James Beard Foundation Outstanding Service Award; four-star Mobil ranking; and the *Wine Spectator*

Grand Award. Tramonto started his culinary career in Rochester, New York, at Wendy's Old-Fashioned Hamburgers in 1977, and has gone on to work with some of the masters, including Pierre Gagnaire, Michel Guerard, and Alfred Portale. Tramonto is an accomplished cookbook author with seven titles to his credit, including his latest, *Rick Tramonto's Steak with Friends*. Tramonto has a history of television work as well, appearing on *Oprah*, the *Today* show, *Iron Chef America*, and most recently as a judge on *Top Chef*.

PHILIPPE TROSCH

Hailing from Biarritz, a resort town on France's Bay of Biscay, Trosch was inspired by restaurateur parents and a grandfather who was a distributor of Bordeaux wine. At age seventeen, he attended culinary school in Normandy and subsequently participated in a program in Paris sponsored by the Cornell University School of Hotel and Restaurant Management. After graduating, Trosch apprenticed at the Ritz Hotel in London and Le Moulin de Mougins, the Michelin three-star restaurant of superchef Roger Vergé. Trosch has worked in great kitchens throughout the world, serving as executive sous chef at the Tamanaco Inter-Continental Hotel in Caracas, Venezuela; chef de cuisine at the Vineyard Room at the Ritz Carlton in San Juan, Puerto Rico; and chef de cuisine at Bernard's, the legendary restaurant at the Biltmore Hotel in Los Angeles. Although his cooking maintains a strong foundation of classic French technique, Trosch's years of experience in diverse locations have inspired the contemporary multiethnic influences reflected in his menus at the Ventana Room where

he worked from 2002 to his recent menus as the executive chef of Chez Colette in the Sofitel Hotel in Philadelphia.

MING TSAI

Ming is the James Beard Award–winning chef and co-owner of Blue Ginger in Wellesley, Massachusetts. Ming and Blue Ginger won the International Facility Management Association's Silver Plate Award in the Independent Restaurant category, recognizing overall excellence in the country. He began his TV career with *East Meets West* (for which he won an Emmy) and *Ming's Quest*. He is the host and executive producer of the public television cooking show, *Simply Ming*, currently in its seventh season. He is also the author of three cookbooks: *Blue Ginger: East Meets West Cooking with Ming Tsai*, *Simply Ming*, and *Ming's Master Recipes*.

Ming is a national spokesperson for the Food Allergy and Anaphylaxis Network (FAAN), and is proud to have worked with Massachusetts Legislature to help write Bill S. 2701, which was recently signed into law. He is also a prolific designer and product developer. His Blue Ginger® Multi-Grain Brown Rice Chips are a hugely popular item in club stores across the nation. Ming is a proud member of Common Threads, the Harvard School of Public Health's Nutrition Round Table, Big Brothers Big Sisters, The Cam Neely Foundation, and Squashbusters.

ELLEN BURKE VAN SLYKE

Ellen Burke Van Slyke has had a long career in the food and beverage world. She owned and operated three restaurants in Tucson, Arizona, including Boccata, which maintains a cult status in the city. She engineered the AAA five-diamond award for the Ventana Room at Loews Ventana Canyon Resort. Currently, she is the corporate director, creative food and beverage, for Loews Hotels.

JULIE TARAS WALLACH
Julie Taras Wallach is the chef and co-owner of two New York City restaurants' Little Giant and Tipsy Parson. Her menus focus on clean, simple flavors and refined reinterpretations of American comfort-food staples. She currently resides in New York City with her husband and fervently believes that "everything tastes better with bacon."

JONATHAN WAXMAN
A successful chef, restaurateur, and author, Jonathan Waxman has graced such prestigious kitchens as Chez Panisse in Berkeley and Michael's in Los Angeles. Waxman went on to open his own restaurant, Jams, in New York City, as well as the famed Washington Park. Today, Waxman is the chef and owner of Barbuto in Manhattan's West Village. His first cookbook, *A Great American Cook*, was published in 2007. Giving back is important to Waxman and he works closely with many charities, including City Meals on Wheels. He currently lives in Manhattan with his wife and three children.

JASPER WHITE
In 1983 Jasper opened his first restaurant, Jasper's, on Boston's historic waterfront. Both the chef and restaurant received numerous awards and were featured extensively in national and local media. In opening his own restaurant, Jasper led a whole new generation of innovative Boston chef/proprietors, many of whom have since gained national prominence. In 1990 Jasper received the James Beard Foundation award for Best Chef: Northeast. After twelve years of being Boston's premier restaurant destination, Jasper's restaurant closed in 1995, and he took time to write two cookbooks, *Lobster at Home* (1998) and *50 Chowders* (2000). His first book, *Jasper White's Cooking from New England*, was published in 1989. In 2007 Jasper released another book, *The Summer Shack Cookbook: The Complete Guide to Shore Food*. In May 2000, Jasper White surprised people who thought he was inextricably linked to fine dining when he opened Jasper White's Summer Shack, in Cambridge, Massachusetts. In July 2009, Jasper opened Summer Shack Express at the new earth Food Court at Mohegan Sun in Connecticut. His most recent Summer Shack, featuring a more subdued and comfortable interior design, opened at the Derby Street Shoppes in Hingham, Massachusetts, in November 2009.

JOE YONAN
Joe Yonan has eaten Rhode Island wieners (don't call them hot dogs), Belgian "barbecue," and Japanese fugu, and once sampled twenty-seven items from twenty-three carts in a five-day street-food extravaganza. But most nights, it's a sweet potato topped with Greek yogurt and a squeeze of lime, or corn tortillas rolled around a fried egg and salsa. Yonan got the cooking bug from his West Texas mother, who let him shop for the family groceries starting at age eight and indulged

his demands to use her stand mixer (a precursor to the KitchenAid). A graduate of the Cambridge School of Culinary Arts, he was a food and travel writer and editor at the *Boston Globe* before moving in 2006 to the *Washington Post*, where he is food and travel editor. He writes occasional features and the monthly "Cooking for One" column for the food section. His work appears in *Best Food Writing 2006* and *Best Food Writing 2007*.

foodbanknyc.org

ABOUT FOOD BANK FOR NEW YORK CITY

Food Bank For New York City is the city's major hunger-relief organization working to end food poverty throughout the five boroughs. The Food Bank mobilizes its efforts through food distribution, direct services, food stamp access, research and policy initiatives, nutrition education, and free tax assistance for New York's working poor. Learn how you can help at foodbanknyc.org.

SHAREOUR STRENGTH®
NO KID HUNGRY

ABOUT SHARE OUR STRENGTH

Share Our Strength is the leading national organization working to make sure no kid in America grows up hungry. By weaving together a net of community groups, activists, and food programs, Share Our Strength catches children at risk of hunger and ensures they have nutritious food where they live, learn, and play. Working closely with the culinary industry, Share Our Strength creates engaging, pioneering programs like Share Our Strength's Taste of the Nation, the nation's premier culinary benefit; Share Our Strength's Great American Bake Sale, a national grassroots effort; Share Our Strength's A Tasteful Pursuit, a touring dinner series; Share Our Strength's Great American Dine Out, a week-long program involving thousands of restaurants nationwide; and Share Our Strength's Operation Frontline, a cooking-based nutrition education program. Visit strength.org and learn more about their goal of ending childhood hunger in America by 2015.

ACKNOWLEDGMENTS

When my friends Laurie and Peter showed me their American flag of bacon and eggs, little did they know the chain of events they were setting off! Their remarkable creation inspired me to approach renowned chefs for their own bacon recipes and was instrumental in obtaining many of the contributors to this book. This book would not be possible without all of the gracious contributors, particularly the fine, bacon-loving chefs and their helpful staffs. A tremendous shout-out to Larry Carrino and the whole team at Brustman Carrino Public Relations, Kate Goldstein-Breyer and the Postcard Communications team, and Lissa Gruman of Gruman & Nicoll Public Relations. All of them recognized the importance of this project and brought it to the attention of the chefs with whom they work. A huge, heartfelt thank-you to my family and friends, specifically Joyce Blau, Beth Rockmill, Tim Nelson, Livia Manfredi, Meg Parsont, Antoine Bootz, Patty Fabricant, and Joe Allegro for their help during the various stages of the book, and for their willingness to talk bacon—and sample recipes—morning, noon, and night. Finally, many, many thanks to the publishing team: Jean Lucas and Kirsty Melville for taking on and supporting the project, Lane Butler for all her hard work, and Ben Fink, Alison Lew at Vertigo Design NYC, and all the behind-the-scenes people, including the sales and marketing team. Everyone who contributed to this book did so to give back to the community and help to abolish hunger in America though the Food Bank for New York City and Share Our Strength. Thank you for believing in me and helping me to deliver this book!

METRIC CONVERSIONS
AND EQUIVALENTS

APPROXIMATE METRIC EQUIVALENTS

Volume

¼ teaspoon	1 milliliter
½ teaspoon	2.5 milliliters
¾ teaspoon	4 milliliters
1 teaspoon	5 milliliters
1½ teaspoons	7.5 milliliters
2 teaspoons	10 milliliters
1 tablespoon (½ fluid ounce)	15 milliliters
2 tablespoons (1 fluid ounce)	30 milliliters
¼ cup	60 milliliters
⅓ cup	80 milliliters
½ cup (4 fluid ounces)	120 milliliters
⅔ cup	160 milliliters
¾ cup	180 milliliters
1 cup (8 fluid ounces)	240 milliliters
1¼ cups	300 milliliters
1½ cups (12 fluid ounces)	360 milliliters
1⅔ cups	400 milliliters
2 cups (1 pint)	460 milliliters
3 cups	700 milliliters
4 cups (1 quart)	.95 liter
1 quart plus ¼ cup	1 liter
4 quarts (1 gallon)	3.8 liters

Weight

¼ ounce	7 grams
½ ounce	14 grams
¾ ounce	21 grams
1 ounce	28 grams
1¼ ounces	35 grams
1½ ounces	42.5 grams
1⅔ ounces	45 grams
2 ounces	57 grams
3 ounces	85 grams
4 ounces (¼ pound)	113 grams
5 ounces	142 grams
6 ounces	170 grams
7 ounces	198 grams
8 ounces (½ pound)	227 grams
16 ounces (1 pound)	454 grams

Length

⅛ inch	3 millimeters
¼ inch	6 millimeters
½ inch	1¼ centimeters
1 inch	2½ centimeters
2 inches	5 centimeters
4 inches	10 centimeters
5 inches	13 centimeters
6 inches	15¼ centimeters
12 inches (1 foot)	30 centimeters

METRIC CONVERSION FORMULAS

To Convert	Multiply
Ounces to grams	Ounces by 28.35
Pounds to kilograms	Pounds by .454
Teaspoons to milliliters	Teaspoons by 4.93
Tablespoons to milliliters	Tablespoons by 14.79
Fluid ounces to milliliters	Fluid ounces by 29.57
Cups to milliliters	Cups by 236.59
Cups to liters	Cups by .236
Pints to liters	Pints by .473
Quarts to liters	Quarts by .946
Gallons to liters	Gallons by 3.785
Inches to centimeters	Inches by 2.54

OVEN TEMPERATURES

To convert Fahrenheit to Celsius, subtract 32 from Fahrenheit, multiply the result by 5, and then divide by 9.

Description	Fahrenheit	Celsius	British Gas Mark
Very cool	200°	95°	0
Very cool	225°	110°	¼
Very cool	250°	120°	½
Cool	275°	135°	1
Cool	300°	150°	2
Warm	325°	165°	3
Moderate	350°	175°	4
Moderately hot	375°	190°	5
Fairly hot	400°	200°	6
Hot	425°	220°	7
Very hot	450°	230°	8
Very hot	475°	245°	9

COMMON INGREDIENTS AND THEIR APPROXIMATE EQUIVALENTS

1 cup uncooked rice = 225 grams

1 cup all-purpose flour = 140 grams

1 stick butter (4 ounces • ½ cup • 8 tablespoons) = 110 grams

1 cup butter (8 ounces • 2 sticks • 16 tablespoons) = 220 grams

1 cup brown sugar, firmly packed = 225 grams

1 cup granulated sugar = 200 grams

Information compiled from a variety of sources, including *Recipes into Type* by Joan Whitman and Dolores Simon (Newton, MA: Biscuit Books, 2000); *The New Food Lover's Companion* by Sharon Tyler Herbst (Hauppauge, NY: Barron's, 1995); and *Rosemary Brown's Big Kitchen Instruction Book* (Kansas City, MO: Andrews McMeel, 1998).

INDEX

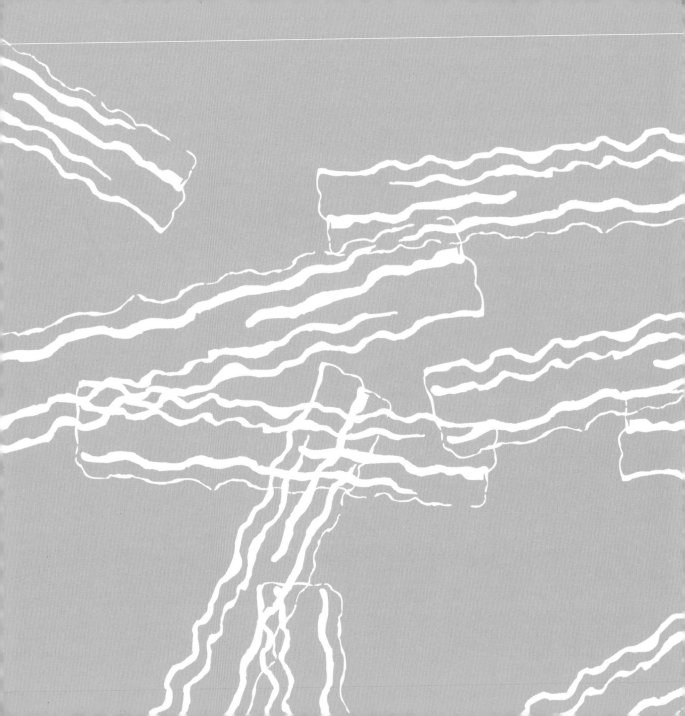